MW00612888

MORE PRAISE FOR *Beware the Purple People Eaters*

"A fantastic read. Dr. Anthony Paustian gives us the road map to personal responsibility and leadership as we define the dash between the years of our life!"

—**BOBBY HANSEN**, retired NBA guard with the World Champion Chicago Bulls

"As a leader, I'm always on the lookout for innovative strategies to improve my own leadership skills and also inspire the imaginations of today's techno-savvy, multitasking, youth-oriented new generation of leaders. Dr. Anthony Paustian's ***Beware the Purple People Eaters*** fits the bill and does it with a motivating flair! I highly recommend this book!"

—**DR. NANCY SEBRING**, superintendent of Omaha Public Schools

"Anthony Paustian's take on personal leadership is the culmination of years of real-world experience as an innovator and educator. He is a doer in every sense of the word, and a walking example of what happens when innovation and action collide. ***Beware The Purple People Eaters*** is a must-read for anyone who wants to lead a better life."

—**ADAM CARROLL**, author of *Winning the Money Game* & *You Don't Know Me from Adam*

"Drawing on personal anecdotes and real-world examples, ***Beware the Purple People Eaters*** offers a metaphor for addressing that which stands in the way of achieving one's potential. Through practical advice gained through personal experience, Dr. Anthony Paustian leads readers through the challenges facing each of us and suggests hands-on approaches for making sensible changes that address our very outlook on life."

—**DR. JASON RHODES**, NASA astrophysicist and cosmologist

Beware the Purple People Eaters

A Personal Look at Leadership

Beware the Purple People Eaters

A Personal Look at Leadership

Anthony Paustian, Ph.D.

Published in Des Moines, Iowa, by BookPress Publishing.

Any requests or questions for the author should be submitted to him directly at tonyp@adpaustian.com.

Readers should be aware that Internet Web sites offered as citations and/or sources for further information may have changed or disappeared between the time this was written and when it is read.

Publisher's Cataloging-in-Publication Data

Paustian, Anthony D., 1964–
Beware the purple people eaters : a personal look at leadership / Anthony Paustian, Ph.D.
p. cm.
ISBN 978-0-9855133-0-6
Includes bibliographical references.

1. Leadership. 2. Creative ability in business. 3. Success in business. 4. Creative thinking
5. Career development. I. Title.

HD57.7 .P38 2012
658.4—dc23 2012906934

First Edition

Printed in the United States of America

10 9 8 7 6 5 4 3 2 1

This book is dedicated to my parents,

Don and Sandy Paustian. Because of their

youthful exuberance, I was brought into the world.

Since that day, I have continued to learn from them.

I couldn't ask for any better example by which to live my life.

I know I don't say it nearly enough, but thanks!

I love you both.

CONTENTS

ACKNOWLEDGMENTS

Thank you to Beth Baker-Brodersen, my editor,
who graciously helped me and is a doer in every sense.

Thank you to David Harrington and Michael Paustian,
who illustrated and designed a fabulous book jacket.

FORETHOUGHT

Outside In.

God made life simple. It is man who complicates it.

– Charles Lindbergh

Ignore the Man Behind the Curtain.

For years now, people have been using the phrase, "Think outside the box." This metaphor has been promoted and reinforced endlessly to encourage us to think in different or unconventional ways or to form different paradigms. The phrase is popular because it espouses an important idea, one that brings with it the appeal of *expression* (it's catchy, easy to remember, and easy to picture—in short, a marketer's dream). But is it time to reexamine the notion? In my various life roles (marketer, college administrator, business executive, designer, writer, professor, husband and father), I've pondered whether it's time to stop and take a look at what was initially in the "box" before everyone decided to start looking outside of it.

My conclusion: some basic "in-the-box" principles seem to have gone by the wayside in our quest to think "outside." These are the very principles which provide a deeply rooted foundation, one which allows us to venture beyond the box and look at things differently if desired, yet enables us to return to the box (and our core values) when necessary. Unfortunately, however, these time-honored values sometimes get lost during the pursuit of what's outside. In virtually all roles, I continue to observe a growing number of people who seem to have little to no awareness of these principles and their ultimate importance and benefit to long-term decision-making and problem solving.

I don't mean to imply that I have lost faith in the future. But, like others before me, my perspective has changed. I remember as a younger person being given advice and guidance by those much wiser: parents, grandparents, mentors and supervisors, not to mention the "authority" figures in pop culture, such as ninja masters or the great Oz himself.

I'm sure—whether consciously or not—I dismissed some of what others tried to impart because I was young and cocky at best, ignorant at worst. Yet these wise people have "been there, done that." They have learned from their mistakes and helped others avoid making the same. Sometimes I believe getting older is nothing more than God saying, "I told you so. You should have listened." I am now becoming one of "those" people—someone who, because of life experiences and the mistakes that come with them, feels compelled to help others (especially my kids) avoid the same mistake-laden path.

I fully understand that much of my new awareness is borne from one person's view based on close to a half-century of anecdotal evidence. But the need to reexamine cultural practices and beliefs (both past and present) has never been greater. It's tempting, I know, to simply assume nothing old works or is acceptable any longer and to dismiss traditional values as just getting in the way of what's new. But we do so at our peril. As Chip and Dan Heath, authors of the best-selling *Made to Stick* observe, "We're always told to think outside the box. But it's about time someone spoke up for the box...Maybe you just need a new one to think in."[1]

So as I sit and straddle the side of my new box (metaphorically speaking), I've written this collection of thoughts as a personal look at leadership. I apologize to the "techies" of the world who might be saddened that I didn't "tweet" the entire collection of thoughts for immediate feed-back. While I appreciate and enjoy the benefits of modern online communication (in all its forms), I wanted to take my time with this process. As you read through these pages, I hope you will find value in the words and reflect on the personal box that currently defines *you* as a leader.

CHAPTER 1

The Invasion of the Purple People Eaters.

Here's to the crazy ones. The misfits. The rebels. The troublemakers. The round pegs in the square holes. The ones who see things differently. They're not fond of rules. And they have no respect for the status quo. You can quote them, disagree with them, glorify or vilify them. About the only thing you can't do is ignore them. Because they change things. They push the human race forward. And while some may see them as the crazy ones, we see genius. Because the people who are crazy enough to think they can change the world, are the ones who do.

– 1997 Apple Computer commercial, "Think Different."

Ah, the Memories.

Sometimes it's funny what you remember from early childhood. I can recall when I was eight and "beaned" directly in the forehead by a baseball while running between two much older kids in a game of pickle; when, at age six, I purchased wax lips and Pixy Sticks at the candy store as I walked home from school; and how my second grade teachers would place me alone in a janitor's closet because I, at age seven, was too disruptive in class. I have often wondered what impact these memories have had, if any, on how I have turned out as an adult.

I realize who I am today is the result of all life experiences, but I can't help but wonder why some memories remain vivid, yet others fade. One memory I recall with great clarity occurred in first grade. My classmates and I were in the middle of coloring time. As I colored a person in my book with a purple crayon, my young, very attractive teacher (whom I also had a serious crush on) leaned over my shoulder and said, "Tony, there's no such thing as a purple person. Could you please use a real skin color for the people?" This comment not only trampled my "manly" self-esteem, it also stifled my creativity (although it did provide an excellent teaching example to use later in life). Even though this experience occurred long before the age of political correctness, my teacher was obviously more concerned my work was correct, rather than different. In short, she provided an example of what I now refer to as a "Purple People Eater," something (usually a person, but also an idea, feeling, etc.) that eats away at the creativity (or Purple People) in others.

They're Everywhere!

The world is full of naysayers: downers with negative attitudes, rule enforcers, priority police, know-it-alls, people fearful of change, and those simply unable to shift their focus of reality. These are the people who continually bombard us with all of the reasons "why not;" those who serve as psychological roadblocks to inspiration, creativity and innovation; and those who continually try to prevent others from doing something different, new, or outside the established boundaries. These Purple People Eaters immediately shoot down ideas with phrases that begin with "You can't," or "It won't."

Make no mistake: I am not an idea zealot. I don't believe in change for the sake of change or in doing something just because it's new. I recognize there are some things that shouldn't necessarily change, especially if no one has created a solution better than the one currently in place. However, until an idea has been fully vetted, this aspect of the equation often goes unknown. As long as people are willing to let others immediately stifle new ideas, there's no way of knowing if the idea or solution is better than the current one. Sometimes, we just don't know until we try.

If Alexander Graham Bell had listened to the naysayers, the telephone might have never amounted to more than just a "parlor toy." If Thomas Edison had listened to people bemoaning his lack of progress while designing the light bulb, I might still be writing this by candlelight. If Henry Ford had listened only to those who were unable to shift their focus, he would have tried to create a "better horse" instead making the automobile affordable for the masses. If Albert Einstein hadn't received the support of Max Planck, recipient of the Nobel Prize in physics, $E=MC^2$ might never have been taken seriously by the physics "establishment;" Einstein could have finished his career as nothing more than a patent clerk. Perhaps I'm being a little extreme here, as the outcomes of their efforts ultimately might have occurred in any case. However, these examples demonstrate that Purple People Eaters are everywhere—always have been, always will be. Avoid them.

Bring On the Purple People.

Two recent studies illustrate my point. Kyung Hee Kim at the College of William & Mary School of Education used Ellis Paul Torrance's studies of creativity assessment to assess American creativity quotient (CQ) scores. Torrance's work, which began in the 1950s and spanned several decades, found that the correlation to lifetime creative accomplishment was more than three times stronger for childhood creativity (CQ) than for childhood intelligence (IQ). Kim then determined that while American IQ scores have been steadily rising with each generation, our CQ scores are trending downward.[1] In a *Newsweek* article, Kim said, "[This downward shift] is very clear, and the decrease is very significant."[2]

Over a span of 16 months, IBM® interviewed more than 1,500 Chief Executive Officers from 60 countries and 33 industries worldwide who identified creativity as the number one "leadership competency" of the future. These CEOs believe that "more than rigor, management discipline, integrity or even vision, successfully navigating an increasingly complex world will require creativity."[3]

Based on these studies, combined with my personal experience as both a leader and a follower, my concern about the future of America's competitive ability in a rapidly changing global economy continues to grow. For more than two centuries, this country steadily led the world in creativity and innovation. Based on patent filings, a widely accepted measure of creativity and innovation, the United States was the dominant leader in global filings—until the 1990s when Japan took over this role, pushing the U.S. into second place.[4] During the early 2000s, China came on strong. From 2003 to 2009, patent filings in the U.S. increased by an average annual rate of 5.5 percent, while China increased 26.1 percent. Recently, U.S. patent filings fell for the first time in 30 years. According to a study by Thompson Reuters, China should become the world's leader in patent filings in the very near future, surpassing both Japan and the U.S. Hence, at least in terms of this particular measurement, China will be considered the world's leader in creativity and innovation.[5]

Why the U.S. decline? Some might say it's the countless hours that children and teens now spend in front of a television absorbing video and playing video games instead of relying on their imagination. Others might say it's the lack of time facing kids today, as they are shuffled from school to soccer to karate classes to flute practice to Cub Scouts. Perhaps it has more to do with how we define creativity, especially the concept of creativity as it relates to early childhood. Everyone is born creative, yet most people probably can't define exactly what creativity is or how it's accomplished. Most will also probably deny they have it. They may often view "creativity" as simply the ability to draw or paint, create music, design houses or products, create movies, or the demonstration of some other tangible outcome, yet true creativity encompasses much more than this limited view.

So What is It?

Within academic circles, creativity has been defined as the creation of something original or useful, or any act, idea, or product that changes or transforms an existing domain.[6] When writing the book *Imagine!*, I defined creativity as "simply a matter of seeing things that everyone else sees while making CONNECTIONS that no one else has made." Creativity through connection-making "is the ability to draw from a variety of sources, pull this information together, and synthesize it" into something new.[7]

Today my definition of creativity has expanded. I have now come to realize that true discoveries seldom happen by "finding" something new but instead are most often simply a matter of people "connecting" what's already there. For example, elements such as oxygen, hydrogen and carbon are some of the building blocks for the physical world. The last element to be found existing naturally in the physical world was Francium in 1939, which was discovered by Marguerite Perey at the Curie Institute in Paris (and it was found to occur naturally only in very trace amounts).[8] Any known element since then has been "synthesized" in a lab through the combination of two or more already known elements. Creativity occurs when people connect things in new ways for different or improved outcomes.

Within the context of business, people have frequently applied this connection-making approach to creativity by continually being on the lookout for novel and interesting ideas used successfully by others. Creativity then occurs when those ideas are adapted to solve problems within specific situations. Helen Barnett Diserens connected the concept of the ballpoint pen to a new method of applying deodorant, the Ban® Roll-On.[9] Fred Smith connected the Federal Reserve check-clearing process to a faster method of shipping, FedEx® Overnight (prior to FedEx, the fastest shipping time was about three days).[10] Steve Jobs (after his return to Apple®) connected the personal computer and consumer electronics to the fashion industry. This not only made computers more appealing through stylish design and the use of color (the iMac®), it turned products like the iPod® into fashion accessories, which people purchase at premium prices. Have you ever noticed how people use Macs in television and film? In part because of his ability to connect consumers to products in distinctive and original ways, Jobs served as the catalyst for today's stylish digital lifestyle.

Bigger is Better.

To successfully connect one thing to another, however, you have to be able to draw from a variety of worlds outside your own. In other words, if you're too heavily focused within a limited context, you won't have any foundation for comparison. Expand your box! You don't need to "get out of the box" to make new connections, just make the box bigger by learning new things, enjoying new experiences, meeting new people, living your bucket list—whatever it takes to expand your horizons while remaining true to who you are. Too often, many of the world's problems can be attributed to people who not only thought they had to "get out of the box," they imagined the box needed to be left behind all together.

Thus they abandoned their values and the foundation of who they truly are.

Three types of people exist when it comes to creative thinking: people who create few, if any, new ideas; people who create new ideas, but do little with them; and people who create new ideas and are able to execute them. I prefer to focus on the third type because ideas really only have value if something is done with them. Thomas Edison once said, "I have far more respect for the person with a single idea who gets there than for the person with a thousand ideas who does nothing."[11]

Edison's statement implies you have to be more than just creative; it is not enough to simply make creative connections. I agree, and I would add two other elements necessary for the realization of a successful outcome: inspiration and innovation. Inspiration is the motivating drive required to initiate creative thinking, and innovation is the process of putting ideas into action, or in other words, using new ideas to add value to existing ones. Edison, who held over a thousand patents, also said, "The value of an idea lies in the using of it."

The Idea Cycle—The Basis for Anything New.

Innovation is actually part of a process, not a singular activity, a process that typically begins with being inspired (motivation), moves into creativity (connection), and ends with innovation (application):

Inspiration takes on many of the same characteristics as basic internal motivation. Being inspired to do something means that future behavior has been given some purpose and direction. This purpose usually has to do with meeting some unmet need or solving a current problem. As with any kind of change, people typically aren't inspired to do something until the pain of their current situation becomes greater than the pain required to change.

Almon Strowger, an undertaker in Kansas City in the late 1800s, exemplifies this concept. The wife of his primary competitor served as the telephone operator and worked the cord board at the local telephone exchange. When callers would request an undertaker, or even Strowger specifically, she would deliberately direct the calls to her husband, Strowger's competitor. Strowger spent years complaining to his local telephone company, but his complaints failed to solve the problem. As a result, Strowger, who really knew very little about current telephone technology, became inspired to solve the problem himself. The result was the invention of the first automated telephone switch, which allowed callers to direct-dial without having to go through a local operator. His inspiration led to a creative solution and resulted in the redesign of the entire telephone industry.[12]

Many examples exist of people outside a particular "establishment" who become inspired to solve a problem, one perhaps others have been unable or unwilling to solve or even identify. John Dunlop, a veterinarian, invented the first pneumatic tire in 1887 to provide a softer ride for his son's tricycle.[13] Leopold Godowsky, Jr. and Leopold Mannes, both musicians, invented Kodachrome® film in 1916 because they felt cheated after seeing the film *Our Navy*, which was advertised as a color film but had extremely poor color quality.[14] Hedy Lamarr, a popular actress during the 1940s, and George Anthiel, a composer, developed a "secret communications system" known as "spread spectrum" technology to help combat the Nazis during WWII. ("Spread spectrum" technology provides the foundation for today's cellular phones and other wireless communications.)[15]

Indeed, almost anyone in any context can become inspired to solve a problem or meet an unmet need. Although the outcomes aren't always groundbreaking, an inspired person must first initiate the creative and subsequent innovative phase of the idea cycle. We all have been, or will become, inspired at some time or another, and this inspiration may not drive an actual creative process. However, creativity seldom exists without inspiration first.

Putting Rubber to the Road.

Have you ever seen or heard an idea and said something such as "I thought of that five years ago" or "I could have done that"? The difference between the idea of something and the actual realization of it is innovation. An "idea" is not enough. You also have to do something with the idea. Innovation is about making new ideas useful—taking the next step to put ideas in action and add value. Edison's idea for the electric light bulb was useless without adequate electricity to power it. For the idea to become useful in everyday life, he had to partner with banker J.P. Morgan to develop a transmission system that allowed electricity to reach homes. The resulting company, General Electric®, became one of the oldest and strongest corporations in the U.S.[16]

Innovation also requires a broader, "bigger picture" perspective which allows us to see relationships, systems, and patterns between ideas, thus enhancing their usefulness. The key to effective innovation is often the ability to manage and coordinate many individual ideas into a singular and unified whole or outcome. One of the greatest modern examples of innovation through the management of ideas would have to be the Apollo Program, which sent twelve U.S. astronauts to the surface of the moon. This program connected the efforts of over 400,000 people from more than 10,000 organizations to create a successful outcome during a time when the lack of technology required an immense amount of orchestrated creativity.[17]

Sometimes the usefulness of an idea isn't always recognized by the creator. In many instances, the ultimate success of an idea may depend on an outsider, one who has been able to observe what the creator could not. For example, the quartz crystal watch was developed in the research labs of the Swiss watch industry (which at the time controlled over 60% of the world market), but Seiko® of Japan and the Hamilton Watch Company of the U.S. developed the idea into a market-changing innovation (one that ultimately eroded most of the Swiss share of the watch market).[18] The engineers at the Radio Corporation of America (RCA) developed the idea for liquid-crystal display (LCD) technology, but it was Sharp Corporation in Japan that turned the idea into a viable product (and something we now take for granted every day).[19]

Where's the Party?

Unfortunately, the word "innovation" today is in danger of becoming a buzzword, just as "paradigm" did in the 1990s and "synergy" did at the beginning of the new millennium. It appears, frequently, in corporate marketing materials, television commercials, investor pitches, and even presidential speeches. People often discuss the importance of innovation and frequently use the word in conversation. However, they also take the true concept of innovation for granted and seldom celebrate it.

True innovators were once heralded as the rock stars of their eras. People would travel from great distances to get a glimpse of Edison's latest invention, the Wright Flyer, one of Tesla's experiments in electro-magnetism, or one of America's first astronauts. World's Fairs (prevalent from 1851-1960s) were designed to inspire, enlighten, and entertain people from all walks of life. In a single location, a World's Fair showcased and celebrated the world's innovations. Today, their luster has diminished, and although they still exist and even draw large crowds, their frequency and attendance have declined. The last fair held in the U.S. was the New Orleans World's Fair in 1984, over a quarter-century ago. Attendance at this fair was less than spectacular (7.3 million compared to 51.6 million for the 1964 World's Fair in New York).[20]

The cultural focus today often seems somewhat misdirected, as a growing emphasis is placed on the tabloid exploits of celebrities, athletes, and the current winner of the "How Can I Be the Most Bizarre and Obnoxious Award" in both music and reality television. Yet innovation has always been a game-changer. It changes how people communicate. It changes how people travel. It changes how homes and businesses operate. It allows people to visit other worlds. It ushered in the atomic age and provides the potential for unlimited energy. It provides food for the growing masses. It adds conveniences and improves the standard of living for many. Innovation has defined this country since its inception. Nonetheless, without a continued focus on innovation and a willingness to take the risks necessary to create it, our country's status and share in world markets will continue to erode and decline.

Our society requires more than just a buzzword to grow and flourish. It requires personal leadership. We are all responsible for innovation which must be a driving force for our future, both collectively and as individuals. And for those who have come before us, the spirit of their innovative efforts should be celebrated, and their stories shared (again and again) to inspire future generations to new creative thought and action.

Fighting Off the Purple People Eaters

- ☐ Most often, you are your own greatest *Purple People Eater*. When do you seem to get in your own way?

- ☐ Document (journal) all of your ideas on a continuous basis whether you "feel" they have any value or not. You never know what the future holds.

- ☐ Create a "sounding board" (1-3 people you can trust) to express your feelings, bounce ideas, vent, whatever. Be open to their feedback, no matter how brutally honest it may be.

CHAPTER 2

Fax Me Up, Scottie!

Computers in the future may weigh no more than 1.5 tons.

– Popular Mechanics Magazine, 1949

To boldly go where no man has gone before.

As a young child in the early '70s, the thought of visiting "other worlds" was the most "groovy" and "far out" thing I could imagine. Who could have pictured humans traveling at many times the speed of light, "beaming" down to mysterious planets, interacting with other species and humanoids, talking through tiny handheld "communicators," collecting data through small "tricorders," firing "phasers," and actually conversing with a female-sounding computer? Of course, none of these scenarios actually existed at the time, but they seemed very real and quite possible, nonetheless, as I watched reruns of *Star Trek* each week on television.

Star Trek originated in the mind of Gene Roddenberry, the show's creator. Roddenberry imagined a totally new universe, one at least remotely plausible yet also grounded in late-1960s science. When Roddenberry conceived of a show where humans travelled throughout the universe, he insisted the show be based on solid scientific concepts. Roddenberry and his team would then visualize the 5th, 10th or 20th generation of what 1960s-era equipment might look like. He insisted that everything on the show be a logical projection into the future (including the multiracial crew). The show stayed scientifically accurate in those things related to the "known process" of space flight (one notable exception was the rate at which people on earth would age in relation to the crew while they travelled at the speed of light) while also remaining accurate in those things necessary to create action, adventure, and entertainment. Thought-provoking storylines related to the social issues of the day. *Star Trek* was also the most expensive show for its time, with complicated plots and high production costs. The weekly television show suffered from extensive budget and time constraints that forced people to new heights of creativity and imagination.[1]

Roddenberry did more than just create a new universe. He also inspired an entire generation of children to become the engineers, scientists, mathematicians, and researchers who would ultimately transform many of the imagined technologies of *Star Trek* into modern-day reality. He inspired women and minorities to take risks and achieve greater success, and he inspired people to envision a world at peace striving to understand its place in the larger scope of the universe.

I was one of those kids. I didn't develop the semiconductor or design the first personal computer, but between *Star Trek* and the Apollo moon missions, I was inspired to visualize what "could be," to apply my imagination, and to develop my creative thinking and innovation skills. Each of these qualities has enhanced my professional and personal life today.

How is Imagination Different from Creativity?

In the last chapter, I defined creativity as simply a matter of "connecting" what already exists in new ways for different or improved outcomes. Through innovation, these creative connections (or ideas) are made useful by taking action. Both concepts are part of the *Idea Cycle* that begins with inspiration, moves to creativity, and finally ends in innovation.

Imagination is the underlying current that flows within the *Idea Cycle*—like a river that carries a raft forward from point A to B to C. It's the ability to visualize that which may or may not actually exist. It's the ability to move a simple concept to a complete idea to a fully realized outcome. Imagination creates mental visuals of abstract ideas and allows for subsequent elaboration of those ideas through future modifications, enhancements, and contingencies. Imagination also

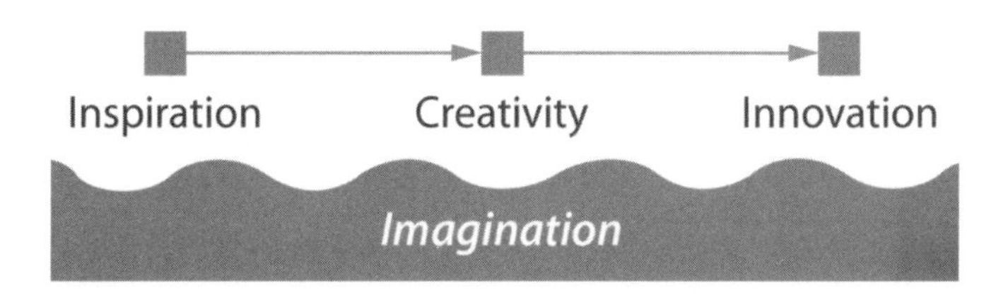

requires personal leadership—a willingness combined with natural desire to visualize something different and take the calculated risks necessary to implement new ideas.

Some argue that it's not truly possible to mentally visualize something without the context of actual experiences or stored mental images. For example, attempt to visualize a red elephant. If you have seen an elephant and recognize the color red, then painting the elephant red (so to speak) in your mind isn't that difficult. For those who have seen the *Star Trek* series or even only its promotion or advertising, most could probably visualize a Vulcan or Klingon from memory. However, what if you were asked to picture a Saurian?[2] Could you do it?

Most of us would probably struggle to visualize that particular alien race, unless we had seen (and could remember) the specific *Star Trek* episode that featured it. Without the memories of specific elements, events or experiences, people often find it difficult to create the mental image of anything outside their personal memories. Yet Gene Roddenberry was able to create the image of a Saurian from scratch. How?

Roddenberry understood that the ability to visualize is a necessary tool for effective creativity and innovation (and the basis for imagination). In order to visualize the first Saurian, he uniquely connected a variety of familiar elements and was able to mentally "see" those connections (the creative process). He was then able to mentally elaborate on those connections, which enabled him to create the storyline and character interaction (the innovative process). Most importantly, he was smart enough to surround himself with other talented, imaginative people who did the same thing. He led his team in a way that allowed imagination to serve as a conduit between creativity and innovation by harnessing the power of visualization.

Every ultimate innovation begins with someone asking "What if" followed by some imagined concept of the future. This ability to imagine begins during childhood and forms the basis for our ability to visualize as adults. When I was young, I built a series of forts. These forts were constructed from lumber, nails, and a variety of other scrap materials scavenged at local construction sites near my home. I would imagine how the fort would look (sometimes sketching it first) and begin building it as I saw it in my mind. Often before I was even finished, I would think of improvements and additions, or conceive of entirely new forts altogether. Once a fort was completed, it was frequently torn apart so construction could begin again. I seldom, if ever, played in them. The satisfaction was more about the process of imagination and accomplishment. I learned construction skills by watching my father around the house and the carpenters at job sites and applied those skills to building ever-better forts. I didn't become an architect or contractor, but this process did enhance my ability to visualize as an adult. We need to allow our children the opportunity to develop this skill on their own through fantasy play and hands-on activities that serve to foster the spirit of imagination.

Does It Really Matter?

Aside from the inspiration, enhanced creativity, and innovative outcomes, imagination is important for a variety of other reasons.

First, the ability to visualize helps us predict the future. Not in a crystal ball, tarot card kind of way, but in ways that help people plan and anticipate what might occur at some future point. Through interaction with the world around us, we are able to envision the occurrence of a future event, based on similar past experiences and events. The result: our ability (or inability) to visualize possible paths will either increase (or decrease) the odds of success.

The Power of the Banana.

My uncle wrestled in college, became a high school teacher, and eventually coached high school wrestling for 17 years. After a two-year hiatus from coaching, the athletic director asked if he would consider becoming the boy's golf coach. (The athletic director was likely a little desperate since the previous coach had resigned suddenly, less than a week prior to tryouts.)

My uncle wasn't a golfer. He knew very little about the sport, and he had a wrestler's mentality—one that was about 180 degrees different from those who golf. After reminding the athletic director of this fact, my uncle was told that his lack of expertise was actually a good thing. By this point, most of the players had already established their games through the private coaching and the guidance of professional golfers at their respective courses. The best thing was to leave them alone to their games and don't try to change them. So my uncle agreed to accept the position.

More than 75 students tried out for the team. Since selection was based on the lowest two-day combined scores, creating a team of 16 players was a relatively easy task. However, the previous coach hadn't earned the players' respect, and my uncle suspected the first practice would be a challenge. He was correct.

They began by hitting balls at the driving range. After a short time, one skeptical senior wanted to see their new coach hit a ball. To avoid being exposed as a golfing fraud, my uncle responded by saying that this wasn't about him, and they needed to focus on their own games. This strategy didn't work, and he could feel an immediate, and growing, lack of respect. Quickly, he walked over to one of the younger boys who had a tendency to slice the ball and told him to move his front foot forward one-half inch (something he just made-up on the spot). Luckily, the boy hit the ball straight as an arrow. Later, on the putting green, he noticed that the senior who had challenged him was missing most of his putts. So, in a voice loud enough for everyone to hear, he said, "John, relax your hands. Your grip is too tight." John luckily sank the next seven putts in a row. My uncle came to the realization that because golf was such a mental game, his sole job was to help these kids avoid letting their minds get in the way of their performance. He ultimately decided he needed to apply some of the same visualization techniques he had once used with wrestlers.

As the team prepared to play for the conference championship, an event the school had not won in over a decade, he could see they were all quite nervous. When they stood up and grabbed their clubs to get out of the team bus, my uncle yelled, "Hey! Who told you to get out? Sit down!" The boys immediately sat. He next reminded them that the school hadn't won this event in a very long time, but "he" knew why. He said, "In the past, this team has been in it to win right up to the last few holes, and then everyone's games started to slide. It's not that anyone lacked the desire to win. Your bodies just started giving out after 15 holes. What you need (pause for dramatic effect)…is potassium! It will lift you up, and I guarantee you will play great for the last three holes." He held up a bunch of bananas, began tossing them at each player, and said, "Bananas, full of potassium, natural steroids, you won't believe how this works. Trust me!" Throughout the match he continued to toss bananas to his players. Before players began teeing off on the 16th hole, he would look at them and say, "Banana." They would look at him and nod.

The boys' golf team won the conference championship. They finished undefeated in duals. They won three additional tournaments. They won the district match. At the end of a highly successful season, they finished second at state (incidentally, this meet was the only one where he had forgotten to bring bananas).

My uncle enabled his team to visualize beyond the moment, beyond the mechanics of their shots, and beyond the spectators. By removing a mental barrier, he helped them to relax before each shot was taken and to see the outcome before it occurred. The imagination and creativity my uncle used to connect wrestling strategies to a totally different sport increased the odds of success for the boys' golf team by helping them to visualize a different path.[3]

You Reap What You Sow.

A little imagination can also greatly raise the bar on outcomes and the ultimate rewards generated by them. Gene Roddenberry's original vision of *Star Trek* resulted in the creation of an entire franchise that to date has included six different television series, eleven motion pictures, a host of fan conventions, and thousands of retail products (not to mention the collector's resale market). The movies alone have grossed more than $1.7 billion worldwide (adjusted for inflation) at the box office.[4]

The children who became engineers, scientists, mathematicians and researchers have gone on to turn many of the technologies that Roddenberry imagined in the late '60s into reality. The cell phones of the late '90s look eerily similar to the tiny handheld "communicators" used by Captain Kirk and Spock. Today's GPS computer systems and the new voice feature of the Apple® and Android® phones sound a lot like the female computer voice on the show. The digital writing pads used by Kirk resemble the first tablet PCs. The digital pads that Captain Packard was often seen reading in the *Star Trek: Next Generation* series (that began in the late '80s) look just like today's iPads® and Kindles®. The video communication between people on the bridge of the Enterprise with those from other worlds or ships seems eerily prescient of today's FaceTime® or Skype®. The earpiece that Lieutenant Uhura used at her station on the bridge of the Enterprise closely resembles my Bluetooth® headset. One could even argue that "beaming" has existed for some time now. No, people aren't getting sent down from the U.S.S. Enterprise to some distant planet, but documents are magically "beamed" through fax machines, and music, art, photos, memos, and a variety of other data are "beamed" daily throughout the world using the Internet.

A Little Pain...Big Gains.

The world of *Star Trek* isn't the only place to demonstrate how investments in imagination can yield positive returns (and sometimes incredible results). Examples can be found in nearly any context:

In 1994, a group of young people used their imaginations to invent the "legend of the Blair Witch," sent three young actors into the woods with video cameras, and created the movie *The Blair Witch Project*. Although the movie's initial production budget was $30,000, the movie went on to gross about $250 million at the box office (not counting the revenue earned through video/DVD sales and sales of merchandise).[5] The movie was listed in the *Guinness Book of World Records* for "Top Budget : Box Office Ratio" (for a mainstream feature film),[6] and since the movie's release, a large number of films have copied its real versus fake concept.

In the late '60s, the idea of looking back at Earth from behind Saturn was the stuff of science fiction and beyond the imagination of many. However, in 2006, the Cassini Orbiter (launched in October 1997) sent back pictures of Earth as seen through the rings of Saturn while the planet eclipsed the sun, thus sheltering Cassini from the sun's blinding glare. A color-exaggerated image was created by the staff at the

NASA Jet Propulsion Laboratory by combining a total of 165 images taken on September 15, 2006 by Cassini's wide-angle camera over nearly three hours. The photo was produced by digitally compositing ultraviolet, infrared and clear filter images and then adjusted to resemble natural color.[7] Similar

Photo Courtesy of Cassini Imaging Team/SSI/JPL/ESA/NASA

photos of earth have been taken by other NASA spacecraft (such as Voyager as it left our solar system), but none so incredible or beautiful as the Cassini images.

And, of course, there's the imagination of the two Steves: the late Steve Jobs and Steve Wozniak (a.k.a. Woz). Woz worked at Hewlett Packard® (HP) designing calculator chips in 1976. When MOS Technology released its 6502 microprocessor that year for $20, Woz could finally afford the chips necessary to design his own computer. He built the machine and displayed it at the Homebrew Computer Club. Based on the excitement expressed by those at the meeting, his friend Steve Jobs convinced him there was a market for the machine (and also imagined a future for personal computers). Since Woz was under contract with HP, anything he designed while under their employ was technically HP property. After showing the computer to the HP executives (and basically being laughed out of the office), Woz quit HP and took what would eventually become the Apple I computer to create a new company with Jobs. Through Jobs's incredible foresight and imagination, Apple would ultimately become the market leader in personal electronics (especially in the area of design) and one of the most valuable companies in the U.S.[8] As Chuck Salter acknowledged in a 2009 *Fast Company* piece, "Apple represents the most successful and faithful marriage of business and design."[9]

Wow! Just Imagine.

During my first computer programming class in college (FORTRAN in the early '80s), students had to write programs and then store/transport those programs on a series of punch cards. Each paper punch card was approximately eight-by-three inches with a pattern of machine-punched holes that represented about 80 characters of data. These cards would be formed into sequentially numbered "decks" to create programs. The card decks would then be fed into a machine that would "read" the cards (the hole patterns) and input the data into a mainframe computer.[10]

As I recently loaded my 16 gigabyte microSD card (about half the size of a small postage stamp) into my digital camera it occurred to me that, 30 years ago, it would have taken about 200 million of those punch cards (no exaggeration) to equal the data capacity of that tiny microSD card (thus defeating the purpose of having a small digital camera in the first place).

My thoughts quickly shifted to Gordon Moore, co-founder of Intel, who was one of the first developers of integrated circuits and silicon chips. In a 1965 issue of *Electronics Magazine*, he authored "Moore's Law," which states that computing power and capacity will double about every 24 months (some believe the number is actually closer to 18 months).[11]

When I contemplate how I once used punch cards to store data and then compare that to what I use today, I can only imagine what wonders await. If we are already seeing many of Roddenberry's ideas coming to fruition now, what lies in the future? If Moore's Law continues to hold true, the computing power we have today will have increased by an amazing 32,768 times in the next 30 years! Who knows, maybe we will see a future like the one imagined in the late 1960s for *Star Trek* (or one even greater) within just a few decades (versus the 23rd century, as originally put forth by the show).

Learn to Visualize.

I frequently talk with people who profess they aren't very imaginative (or that they have difficulty with visualization). I believe the problem is a matter of "don't" versus "can't." Just as the average person cannot roll off the sofa to run a marathon without proper training, the ability to visualize requires preparation, practice, and the discipline to push your mind off its nice, comfy "couch." A number of strategies and activities can improve your ability to visualize, and hence, your level of imagination:

• **Daydream.** In a *Psychology Today* piece discussing studies using brain-scanning technology, researchers have found a significant correlation between robust daydreaming and superior intelligence. Their findings indicate the state of daydreaming was far more active in the "superior intelligence group" than in the "average intelligence group" in those studied. In other words, allowing one's thoughts to bounce around between the past, present and future while accessing stored knowledge creates stronger memories and experiences. Apparently, those with superior intelligence "allow" this process to occur, thus enabling them to yield greater insights as a result. Many smart people—from Einstein to Mozart—have credited these insights and their imagination as the source of their intelligence.[12] To enhance the benefits of daydreaming, you must allow time for it, acknowledge it when it's happening, and even take notes for later reference. My greatest daydreaming periods occur while I'm driving, running, and lying in bed before falling asleep. Knowing this, I always keep pen and paper (others may use their smart-phones) nearby in case an especially promising idea comes to mind.

• **Learn New Things.** The process of "making connections" requires an ever-growing base of information and stored knowledge available for the mind to access. Imagination and visualization are no different. Since the ability to "picture" new things in your mind often depends on mentally "altering" things you already know (think red elephants), an ever-growing, diverse base of knowledge and personal experience will greatly enhance your visualization skills. As the marathoner does, hop off the couch and experience the world around you. A mind once stretched by a new thought, experience or memory never returns to its original shape or dimensions.

• **Learn to Focus.** I'll never forget when I took my daughter to see the IMAX® movie *Hubble*. The movie featured one of the space shuttle's missions to repair the Hubble telescope while in orbit and featured a number of the breathtaking images of the cosmos taken by Hubble. Viewed on the immense IMAX dome screen, the movie seemed larger than life, and it captivated my 17-year-old daughter's attention. She was engaged and even asked questions—for about 15 minutes—until she received a text message and some new Facebook updates (and then she was gone). In a world today where it seems many of us lack the ability, or the inclination, to focus on any one thing for very long, it's no wonder we struggle to visualize new things.

It's tempting to rationalize this lack of sustained attention by focusing on how much we "accomplish" through technology, for instance. Yet, to some degree at least, our attempts to multitask our way through life appears to have resulted in a bunch of things getting done, but with a lesser degree of quality. Sometimes watching my kids, their friends, and the multitude of college students I come in contact with every day is like watching one giant case study in attention deficit disorder fueled by an ever-growing market for specialized energy drinks. Markets typically reflect changes in culture, and a recent scan of these drinks at the local convenience store yielded over 20 brands with names like *Monster*®, *Full Throttle*®, *Wired*®, *Nuclear*®, *Amp*®, and *Venom*®. This behavior isn't all that different from when I was in college, but our options—and the extent to which students relied on them—was limited. Our choices then typically included Mountain Dew®, No-Doze®, and good 'ole coffee to help keep us awake and alert. Today, instead of focusing on one thing at a time and doing it well, people often seem to seek whatever boost they can get to maintain their energy levels in order to do many things not quite as well. Learn to focus.

• **Ask.** The following questions can help us begin to "see" the context and bigger picture of almost anything, as well as how the various pieces connect to form the whole:

- Why?
- What if?
- What would that look like?
- Why not?
- What would it take?

In order to understand and learn, young children master the art of continuous questioning. As we grow older, this process can also help us foster our ability to visualize.

A Treasure Map of Opportunity.

Imagination provides the mental canvas for creativity and innovation to occur which ultimately allows us to visualize how everything fits together. This underlying ability to visualize how things connect (process of creativity) enables us to elaborate on those connections (process of innovation) in the same mental space. By opening our imagination, the possibilities become endless.

Leadership, personal or otherwise, provides direction and a path towards the successful completion of something that adds value. An active imagination will help guide that process by uncovering opportunities and revealing new worlds previously unimagined or unrealized.

The imagination behind *Star Trek* inspired an entire generation to seize available opportunities. Dr. Marc Rayman, chief propulsion engineer at NASA's Jet Propulsion Laboratory, was motivated by the *Star Trek* episode, "Spock's Brain," to develop ion propulsion for deep space probes. Ion propulsion, based on electrically charged atomic particles, is ten times faster than that based on traditional rocket fuel. Martin Cooper, chief engineer at Motorola® and inventor of the cell phone, credits *Star Trek* and its mobile "communicator" for his inspiration. Dr. Mae Jemison, inspired by *Star Trek's* Lieutenant Uhura, the African-American communications officer and full member of the Enterprise bridge crew, became the first African-American woman in space. While in orbit in the space shuttle Endeavor, Jemison opened all of her communication sessions with Uhura's famed statement, "All hailing frequencies open." Dr. John Adler, a neurosurgeon at the Stanford School of Medicine, admits he was thoroughly inspired by Dr. McCoy's non-invasive techniques used in the Enterprise sick bay. He invented the CyberKnife Radiosurgical System, a computer-controlled laser that noninvasively ablates tumors and lesions throughout the body (Adler also holds nine United States patents in the fields of surgery, medical imaging, and therapeutic radiation). Ed Roberts invented the Altair 8800, a kit computer which had to be assembled by the purchaser (and led to Bill Gates forming Microsoft®). Roberts named the computer after the solar system Altair 6 from the *Star Trek* episode "Amok Time."[13] And the list goes on.

As it has throughout time, imagination transforms the world at record speed and shows no signs of slowing. Computers continue to evolve into machines ever more powerful, smaller, dispersed, and increasingly connected. If computing power continues to increase at exponential rates as Moore predicted, an active imagination—and the ability to visualize—will remain among the most important and vital leadership traits required to generate successful outcomes (and possibly create a future thus far unimagined today).

Fighting Off the Purple People Eaters

- ☐ Reconsider your surroundings. How do the people around you and your work/home environment impact your ideas and the outcomes of solutions to problems?

- ☐ What people in your life are the most supportive? Spend more time with them. What people in your life aren't very supportive? Spend less time with them.

- ☐ Allow yourself time to do nothing except daydream. If you have to go to some kind of "special place" in order to relax, do it. Remember to write down all of your ideas and thoughts.

- ☐ Don't assume! Ask LOTS of questions—like a young child who constantly asks, "Why?" This will often help you get to the root reason for anything and help you to better understand the cause driving it.

CHAPTER 3

Attack of the Killer Kirby.

You can always find a distraction if you're looking for one.

– Tom Kite, PGA Golfer

That Really Sucks!

I remember the first vacuum cleaner that I purchased back in the late 1980s—an eight pound Oreck® upright. It was compact, lightweight, and easy to use. Based on my income at the time, it also wasn't cheap, and it took time to pay it off. That vacuum worked great, and I owned it for many years. Then one day there was a knock at my door. It was a Kirby® salesman. In a world which features the personal computer and the Internet, it's hard to believe that door-to-door salespeople still exist, yet there he was, vacuum in hand. At first, I thought it was something that was being delivered to my house by mistake. But after some smooth talking on his part, there he stood, in my living room, dumping a full cup of sand all over my carpet.

Before I even had a chance to complain, he asked if he could use my current vacuum to clean it up. I proceeded to get it out of the closet, and he started vacuuming until we both seemed convinced that my trusted Oreck had done its job. Then he whipped out the Kirby (with a special clear canister instead of a bag so we could clearly see what was being sucked up) and vacuumed the same spot again. I couldn't believe what I was seeing; the Kirby had sucked up a lot of sand that my vacuum had missed. And like the sand in the clear container, I was sucked right into buying the Kirby on the spot (and it proceeded to vacuum out my wallet as it was considerably more expensive than the Oreck). Cost wasn't an issue though—especially in light of what I had just witnessed.

The Suction of Vacuums.

I believe this story illustrates a common problem today. With the rapid pace of daily life (which only seems to be accelerating), people often get caught up in what I call "focus vacuums." A vacuum, by definition, is the absence of matter (or a Kirby if you like). Nature abhors vacuums and does whatever it can to fill the empty void with whatever immediately surrounds it.

As an avid observer, I have noticed a growing tendency in which people allow the "stuff" in their daily lives to suck them in like giant vacuums. A personal vacuum occurs when one's thought process becomes overly focused on a specific situation or event (like dumping sand onto my carpet). We sometimes focus most heavily on the here-and-now and whatever specific situation we are dealing with at the time, thereby missing the big picture. We seem overwhelmed by the many "details" of our lives and try to balance everything with the hope of being successful and happy. Our energy gets divided into small bits, spread over a large number of simultaneous actions, instead of allowing us to focus on being efficient, productive and successful within the larger scope of the activity. Individual activities themselves seem to have a higher priority than the holistic nature of them, and as a result, people often find it more difficult to make everything work together towards one common purpose and something greater for the long-term. The suction of vacuums has a direct, negative impact on our ability to visualize anything new, better, or different.

For example, think back over your life. Can you remember a past event which, at the time, seemed so overwhelming or troublesome that you had no idea how you were going to deal with it, let alone survive it? How about that breakup with your first love or when you were laid off from your job?

Throughout the latter part of my high school years, I dated someone I would define as the "first love" of my life. She was a girl who, as far as I was concerned, could do no wrong. However, my parents didn't quite see her in the same way, and my mother would often refer to her as "poison" because (in my mother's view at least) she was poison to my ability to make rational, mature decisions. My mother's perception only served to entrench my feelings toward my girlfriend of course. When we eventually broke-up after a few years, I was devastated; it affected every aspect of my life. I didn't feel like eating, leaving the house, or doing anything, for that matter. I remember sitting in my bedroom for hours listening to the Styx song "Babe" over and over. It was the end of life as I knew it.

Eventually, though, I got over it. Later I realized that not only was my mother right (I had indeed made some very poor decisions), I had allowed my relationship and the subsequent break-up to divert me well off the course I had earlier set for my life. The worst part was I had no idea I had gotten off-track until it was too late. "Poison" had become a vacuum in my life that sucked all of my energy and diverted my focus.

Vacuum events are sort of like the black holes of the universe. They require mass amounts of energy and shift our focus away from the long-term to everything short-term and immediate. In hindsight, they are seldom as big of a deal as we made them out to be, especially in the context of life's big picture. More often than not, we are ultimately able to survive and move past them, and we probably became a better person as a result.

Because the distractions in our lives seem to be increasing at an exponential rate, I see vacuums having an ever-growing impact. People spend so much time dealing with such a large number of little vacuums, they become bogged down like a car stuck in mud. When living in a world of vacuums, we become overly focused on specific details without stopping to contemplate the potential long-term impact. We sometimes get sucked into believing that everything is equally important, which distorts reasoning and keeps us from seeing how specific situations or problems fit into the overall scheme of things.

Vacuums are the archenemy of productivity and goal-directed behavior. Vacuums work overtime to divert the thought process down some unproductive mental tunnel, and if allowed, they can choke the process of achieving goals like weeds in a garden. The effective personal leader is very conscious of the negative effects caused by vacuums and fights hard to resist their sucking power of distraction. The greatest guard against vacuums is conscious direction guided by the power of a tangible vision.

The Suction Blocker.

Throughout life we are confronted by countless problems to solve and decisions to make. Some are extremely important, yet most are relatively insignificant and fruitless. Some will require a rapid decision while others pose no real time constraints. Some carry a high level of risk while others are risk-free. Some are complex while others are fairly simple and effortless.

However, regardless of the problem to solve or decision to make, the only way to maintain a sense of focus as to what is truly important (and avoid the vacuum effect) is to maintain a tangible sense of vision. This vision allows you to create and maintain daily perspective, thus providing you the power to resist and fight off the continuous daily suction of vacuums we all face.

Allow me to illustrate. One thing is true in terms of human behavior—over the long-term, people's behavior will ultimately align with their personal values. In other words, although people will routinely compromise values in the short-term for a variety of reasons, eventually their behavior will shift towards that (whatever "that" might be) which they deem to be most important within their lives. In my case, it was life itself.

In the fall of 2008, I went for my routine annual physical. Everything was fine except for a bad liver score on my blood test. Under "normal" circumstances, my physician said he wouldn't have been too concerned about it since a couple of mixed drinks consumed shortly before the blood test would have caused a similar spike in the test. One problem, however: I didn't drink.

To be safe, he ordered an ultrasound of my liver, and the test confirmed what he had suspected. I had non-alcoholic fatty liver disease.

He told me that the condition was more than likely the result of bad genes and not anything that I had necessarily done, like overeating. Please understand, I wasn't "fat" in the traditional sense, but I also didn't give a second thought to what I put into my mouth. I was so busy living each day that, like most people, I ate a bunch of fast food and didn't exercise very much. Over time with age, my weight slowly crept up to the point where I could easily stand to lose a few pounds, like maybe five or so (at least that's what I thought).

During my next visit, my physician shared both the facts of the disease and the only known effective treatment according to most studies; I had to lose 10-15% of my body weight. In other words, he wanted me to lose about 35 pounds before my next annual physical!

In order to achieve such a daunting goal, I knew I needed a tangible vision of what the future looked like if I wanted any chance of making changes to my daily behavior. I knew I wasn't going to lose the weight overnight, especially since I spent years putting it on. I needed something that I could strive for—something I could put in front of me at all times to remind me why I had to stay away from fast food, sweets, junk food (basically anything that tasted good), and why I would be having to sweat so much on my treadmill.

I could have easily picked a photo of some young "ripped" guy like those featured in exercise equipment commercials, but I knew that wasn't realistic for me. I needed real.

The Inspiration.

So, I picked three photos: one of a fatty liver, one of Jared (a 450-pound college student before he started eating Subway®) and one of Jared after he dropped a couple hundred pounds doing it.

Jared's father, a physician, finally used fear as a tactic and basically told Jared that if he didn't lose weight, he wouldn't live past 35. Jared was so large that he chose his course schedule in college based not on the courses he wished to take or who was teaching them, but instead on which rooms had tables that would facilitate his enormous body. He started eating a foot-long veggie sub at lunch and a six-inch turkey sub at night. He lost 100 pounds in three months. After that he began to walk more and the weight started coming off even more quickly.[1]

Each day I looked at all three photos to remind me of what I was trying to achieve and to help keep me focused on the purpose behind all of my "suffering." I also studied all of the current diets that were available, and after reading the summary of a Harvard University long-term study on diets, I decided that my best course was to just "eat less" and exercise. I committed myself to eating no more than 2000 calories per day with regular weekly exercise until I lost the weight and then increase my calorie intake to 2500 daily once I reached my goal. I kept a journal of both calories burned through exercise and the calorie count of everything I ate to ensure I was staying within my daily goal (and to help me resist the countless vacuums that regularly appeared, like the cookies brought into the office or the cheesecake sitting in front of me at one of the many event dinners I attended).

The result: I lost 45 pounds in four months. I have since stopped keeping written track of ingested and burned calories. However, having done that for a few months, I managed to memorize most calorie amounts in foods and to this day keep a running total in my head in order to consume about 2500 calories or less daily. I have been able to keep off the weight because the short-term changes to my daily behavior patterns resulted in relatively permanent changes in my lifestyle. As a result, I am able to resist getting sucked in by food vacuums (although I admit I occasionally cheat now and then, especially on holidays).

Granted, to a certain degree I was motivated by fear (since my physician basically said to either lose the weight or die). But I was also motivated by the value I had for my life. Whether it's life, family, employees, finances, God or country, understanding that which we value or feel to be the most important helps us create a personal tangible vision that will result a greater likelihood of the ability to take control of daily activity and achieve long-term success.

Ultimately, the secret to achieving what you want, regardless of your situation in life, comes down to two things:

- Keep a picture of what you want in front of you at all times to serve as a constant reminder, and
- Make daily choices that reflect the values represented by that picture.

Like most things in life, success is achieved by the daily decisions we make over time, not the decisions made in a single day.

Fighting Off the Purple People Eaters

- ☐ What shapes your current "box"? What obstacles—such as fear, insecurity, financial constraints, or some other self-imposed limitation—get in the way of expanding it? Look deeper and be honest with yourself. Otherwise you can't fix whatever holds you back.

- ☐ What makes you feel uncomfortable? Why? Face obstacles head on.

- ☐ Simplify your life. Simplicity provides greater certainty and decreases stress.

CHAPTER 4

Haste Makes Waste.

The only reason for time is so that everything doesn't happen at once.

– ALBERT EINSTEIN

Nuts!

When I was a little boy, go-karts were all the rage in my neighborhood, and many of the kids had great-looking karts that their dads had noticeably spent a bunch of time constructing. Obviously, I too wanted a kart that I could push around and ride down the hill near our house. The road on the hill was paved with a tar and pea-sized gravel surface (I guess roads are no longer covered this way for environmental reasons).

When I asked my dad to help me build a kart, he proceeded to take one large board, slap a couple of smaller boards to the bottom of it in order to hold the axles and wheels (the front board was able to pivot), and place a rope on both ends of the front board to be used for steering.

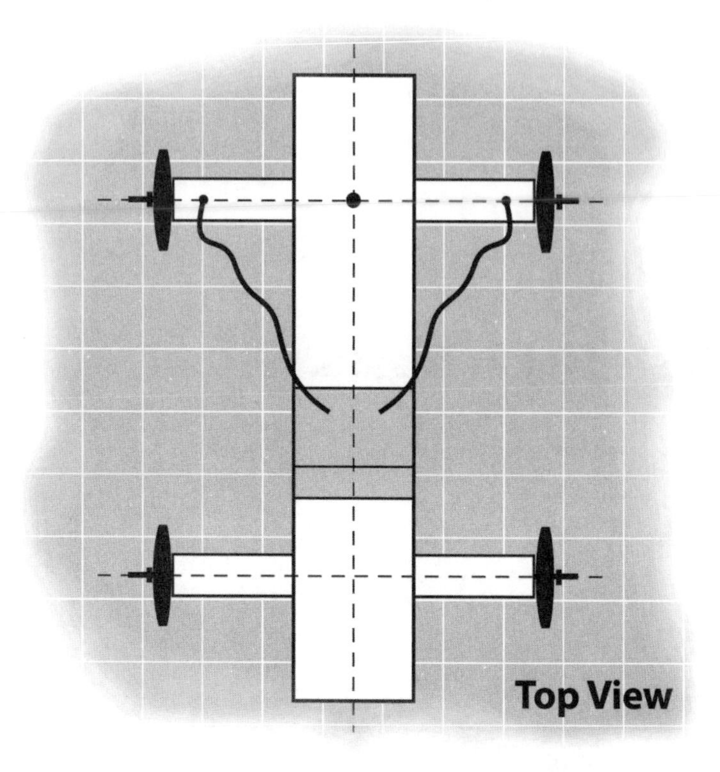

Needless to say, my dad wasn't too worried about visual aesthetics and was far more concerned about getting me started with my "new ride" (ironically, if he built a kart for me today it would probably look like a Formula One Indy Car made of wood). However, there was one major flaw in my dad's rapid design; he used completely threaded steel axles that extended a few inches beyond each end of the smaller boards with large threaded nuts to hold on the wheels. It seemed like a good idea at the time and an easy way to attach the wheels. However, each time I took the kart to the top of the hill and proceeded to let gravity do its job, the spinning wheels would gradually unscrew the nuts from the axles and one or more of the wheels would come off while the kart was in motion. You can picture the rest.

My dad is one of the smartest people I know, and an exceptional craftsman when it comes to building furniture and doing many other hands-on projects. Granted, the kart construction occurred about 40 years ago before he had fully developed his skills, but this isn't a story about skill. It's a story about haste and not completely thinking through the long-term outcomes of very short-term actions.

Throughout my entire childhood, my mom used the phrase "Haste makes waste!" to emphasize what would happen if I rushed something or was more concerned about hurrying through tasks rather than doing them correctly. Her intention was to get my brother, sister, and me to slow down, take our time, and do our best job on whatever we were doing at the time.

I now realize how almost comical our lives have become today as we try to cram as much activity as possible into a finite amount of time. We justify this busyness as "multi-tasking," and the result is a life filled with added undue stress, a growing lack of long-term focus, and a resulting decrease in long-term effectiveness. I regularly see people working frantically each day, performing tons of tasks and activities, expending a bunch of energy, and yet seeming to accomplish very little of significance before becoming frustrated.

Want Fries with That?

People are so busy being busy that we have nearly created a total "take-out" existence. Our expectation is to do ever more while achieving instant response and gratification. With changes in technology, delivery systems, and social norms, we now live in a take-out culture:

- automatic teller machines and real time online banking
- pay-at-the-pump gas
- instant credit approvals for purchases (that you may or may not be able to afford)
- pills to rapidly fix a host of physical or psychological problems
- fast food with drive-up windows or rapid delivery
- even more drive-up windows in pharmacies, dry cleaners, liquor stores, banks, coffee shops, bakeries, and grocery stores
- same-day and overnight delivery services
- e-mail, voicemail, text messaging, tweeting, and the smartphones that facilitate it all
- "hanging out" with friends on social media sites and blogging about all of it from your sofa
- online and downloadable movies, music, television, and virtually all other forms of entertainment without leaving your house (or sofa)
- expedited checkout and ordering through barcode scanning
- web-based education
- 10-minute oil changes
- virtual reality
- schemes for rapid weight loss, quick wealth accumulation, and fast exercise routines

- instant bill pay
- complete microwavable meals made in seconds
- 8-minute speed dating events and online dating services

And the list of life-accelerating examples goes on and on. With the growing rate of "now" in our lives, one thing is becoming increasingly clear: we now live in a society where flexibility, immediacy, and instant gratification have become the norms in life. So much so that I've come to think of the youth of today as the "generation of instant", or iGen (to borrow the "i" from Apple®).

Notice those around you. Many people today seem to have very little patience, complain when they don't have enough time to do everything, have shorter attention spans and a lack of focus, and expect change or things to happen quickly. As a result, these same people don't seem as willing to allow initiatives to play out until the end, don't seem as willing to make decisions that may require considerable time to accomplish, and don't seem as willing to focus long enough to complete a goal. At the very least, as my mother would say, it's haste making waste.

Having taught undergraduate and graduate college courses and having held a variety of leadership positions for over 25 years, I've witnessed a growing discontent and frustration by people concerning the lack of time they have to complete tasks. Almost daily, I hear people complain about not having enough time to do everything. But I can't help but think, "Don't we all have the same amount of time—24 hours per day, 7 days per week, 52 weeks per year?"

Since time moves the same for everyone, then what it really comes down to are choices, priorities, and vacuums. People ultimately choose what they will do and prioritize the order in which it will be done, yet they still allow vacuums to distract them from staying on course. (Remember, a personal vacuum occurs when one's thought process becomes overly focused on a specific situation or event.)

Personally, I'm no different than anyone else. My life sometimes seems to blur together without real distinctions between work, home and play. I get frustrated by flight delays, Internet delays, slow computers, slow drivers, slow customer service, and pretty much anything else that either delays or slows me down. However, one area where I have made considerable progress is in the area of decision-making. Because of many poor past decisions, I have now become very aware of my time and more proactive with how I use it.

In order to be effective in the long-term, I have had to get control of my short-term DAILY activity. I now force myself to stop and ask, "Why am I doing this (or that) and what purpose does it serve?" I have learned to:

- become very conscious of how I use my time as it is very precious and not unlimited;
- become very conscious of vacuums and how they, more than anything else, can continually pull me away from what I truly want to achieve;
- minimize all of the extraneous "stuff" in my life and especially those activities which don't help me reach my ultimate goals;
- work at a slower, more thoughtful pace, which

actually makes me more effective, and focus on one thing at a time to minimize the multitasking.

All of these decisions have helped to improve the quality of my work.

Impact on Leadership.

Our take-out, instant gratification culture has also complicated the role of leaders. Leadership, personal or otherwise, is all about the quality of decision-making, and one of the biggest decisions that leaders face is long-term success versus short-term gain. As more leaders are now being evaluated on shorter-term outcomes, the temptation is to make decisions that reflect greater short-term gains regardless of how those decisions may or may not affect the long-term.

In other words, to steal a phrase I once heard from a friend and college basketball coach, "You're only as good as your last season." Since people have less patience, we as leaders, both personal and organizational, are being asked to show rapid, short-term gains that once took much longer to accomplish. Whether you're a coach, politician, CEO, president, sales manager, church pastor, or simply a parent, a growing pressure exists to exceed short-term expectations, unrealistic or otherwise, in whatever manner possible. The result is often rapid success or positive outcomes, followed by a downturn of some manner in the years beyond.

For example, in 1997, Jim Leyland, a very talented baseball coach, was hired by owner Wayne Huizenga to coach the Florida Marlins, a team that was only in its fifth year of existence. With a number of very talented players ("purchased" for a total of $89 million, one of the highest team payrolls in the league at the time), Leyland was able to coach the Marlins to the World Series and the expansion franchise's first championship. Immediately following that great season, Huizenga claimed he was losing millions of dollars and immediately began to dismantle the team in what became known as the "great fire sale." As a result, Leyland had a terrible 1998 season and resigned soon thereafter.[1] This example illustrates that with enough short-term effort or investment, great short-term outcomes can be achieved. However, without a solid basis or foundation built on a strategic focus, sustaining positive outcomes is difficult, if not impossible.

When Haste Doesn't Make Waste.

Up to this point, I have primarily focused on effectiveness in long-term decision-making. However, the aspect of efficiency is also just as important, and there are times when taking a short cut or accelerating a process can actually yield long-term positive results. While effectiveness can be viewed as "making right decisions," efficiency would then be viewed as "minimizing the amount of required resources."

Like the phrase that Nike® coined in 1988, sometimes the best strategy is to "Just Do It"—just jump in and get the job done because that is what needs to happen. Yet many people will delay making decisions because of the risk associated with uncertainty. As long as this short-term process has been thought through in the context of a long-term strategy (and this is key), decision-making can yield a greater level of efficiency by using less time, money, and other valuable resources. We are able to accelerate the process of accomplishing desired long-term goals and objectives through more rapid, yet effective, short-term decision-making.

When a child is taught how to ride a bicycle, she usually gets a bike with a set of training wheels to support the bike during the learning process (or at the very least, the child is placed on the bike while a parent runs along the side holding it steady). Over time, the parent will gradually inch up the training wheels until the point where the child is no longer using them. This is typically followed by a grand ceremony of taking off the training wheels in front of the child as if she had just "graduated."

For whatever reason, my dad decided that an expedited, more direct approach would be better. On that same freshly-tarred hill where I rode my go-kart, my dad took me to the top, placed me on the bike, and let me go. Of course, I didn't stay on it very long and fell. Dad just picked me up, brushed off the sticky gravel, placed me back on the bike, and let me go again. We repeated this process until I was riding on my own. Needless to say, I caught on quickly. I either had to learn how to ride or endure the pain of repeatedly falling and becoming "tar and graveled."

I'm not sure how much time my dad spent thinking through this "teaching moment" (which some people today might find somewhat harsh), but his actions had a huge impact on how I approach and deal with goals, tasks and obstacles. Instead of slowly and incrementally approaching them, I have a tendency to more quickly size-up a situation, make a decision, and jump on the bike (so to speak). But unlike speed for the sake of speed, he taught me that the most efficient path to success sometimes can be the quickest, but also the hardest, because it requires determination and a willingness to endure short-term pain for long-term gain.

Change is seldom easy. To facilitate it, we should identify and empower those who are willing to jump in and try, and then work with these people to accomplish desired goals and objectives. This will actually serve to improve and motivate those around us (as well as raise the level of expectation for everyone).

Of course, I've made mistakes and poor choices, just like everyone else. However, I have come to realize that this one simple teaching moment actually had less to do with learning to ride a bike and far more to do with providing me a greater lesson, as I now possess the tools and drive to be more proactive and determined to succeed at whatever I'm doing.

So whether intentional or not, thanks for the lesson, Dad. And thanks for the go-kart too. A simple kart, even one with a flawed design, was much better than having no kart at all.

Fighting Off the Purple People Eaters

- ☐ When and where do you feel the most motivated? Go there.

- ☐ Change it up. Learn and do different things. (Get out of your normal routine and especially that big hole called the comfort zone.)

- ☐ Recall a situation when you felt complete peace and harmony. What about it made you feel that way? Duplicate it whenever possible.

CHAPTER 5

Noses, the Grindstone, and a Guy Named Kurt.

If a man is called to be a street sweeper, he should sweep streets even as Michelangelo painted, or Beethoven composed music, or Shakespeare wrote poetry. He should sweep streets so well that all the hosts of heaven and Earth will pause to say, here lived a great street sweeper who did his job well.

– Martin Luther King, Jr.

The Entitlement of Opportunity.

As a child, I was taught to strive for the American Dream, which was something you could "earn" through hard work and persistence. It wasn't something simply received because you were an American (hence the word "Dream"); the only aspect of the American Dream a citizen was actually entitled to was the opportunity to work hard for it. People who migrated to this country understood the hard work necessary for achievement and believed it was worth the sacrifices. The opportunity to work hard for something of one's own inspired the high levels of motivation needed to succeed.

Yet when I compare things today to past attitudes about hard work, achievement, and citizenship, something seems amiss. Today it feels as if a growing number of people simply just feel entitled to the Dream or some portion of it without having to put in the required work. Many conversations and discussions with employers, educators, and fellow workers over the years have led me to think that somehow things have changed. Combined with the flourish of news and media-related stories about the growing levels of entitlement and programs which support that concept, it's easy to believe there is a declining individual work ethic that touches all types of people and all levels of employment.

I grew up in a typical middle-class home where my parents often said things like, "Whatever you do, put your all into it," or "If you borrow something from someone, always return it in better condition than you received it." Their actions reflected these views; they walked the talk and taught by example. These mini-lessons on work ethic throughout my childhood became the mortar that formed the foundation of who I am today. Keeping my "nose to the grindstone" became the mantra of my personal life.

As a teenager, I had numerous hobbies, interests, and lofty dreams, combined with a strong desire for success. Yet my interests and plans required money I didn't have and somehow needed to earn. So I did whatever I had to do, such as mowing lawns, detasseling corn, picking tomatoes, babysitting, bagging groceries, painting, washing cars, selling nails (picked up from the ground at construction sites—with permission—after they were dropped), and even selling fireworks. (My friend and I would purchase fireworks in Missouri, where they were legal, and bring them back to Iowa, where they weren't so legal. We would then sell them at a considerable profit. Although we ultimately did get in a little trouble with the police, one has to admire our teenage entrepreneurial spirit.) This same "work ethic" also carried over into my schoolwork, which resulted in very good grades made possible by meeting and exceeding the amount of assigned work.

Today, when I think about work ethic, I have to ask what it means now and how it fits into people's lives. According to The *American Heritage Dictionary of the English Language*, work ethic is defined as "a set of values based on the moral virtues of hard work and diligence."[1] However, the term "moral virtues" seems to imply a sense of universal understanding as to the meanings of both hard work and diligence. People can be very busy, working very hard for a long period of time, yet really do nothing of value to improve their lives or help them obtain the "American Dream" as they perceive it. However, according to the stated definition, they still might be viewed as having a strong work ethic despite the outcomes. But do they really?

A Slightly Different View.

I have an alternate definition, one I believe captures the essence of work ethic. To me, work ethic can be defined as simply "doing whatever you need to do in order to get whatever you want." When people persistently, and consistently, do all of the things necessary in order to reach a desired level of personal success, they will exhibit the degree of work ethic required to get there. For example, if someone is content making $20,000 per year by steadily working a full-time job that pays $10 per hour, then that person would be exhibiting the required level of work ethic to achieve this desired level of success.

Although others may not agree that this person exhibits a strong work ethic, success is a very relative term, and its definition often depends upon the views of the person evaluating it. Many variables go into one's personal view of success that might run contrary to the view of society at large. The key is to realize that as long as you do whatever you need to do in order to get whatever you want (achieve your desired level of success), you are exhibiting the necessary degree of work ethic regardless of what others may think. However, when people desire something more, something they currently don't have, or their expectations of success increase, they must work harder to achieve this higher level of "want," and thus exhibit a stronger work ethic.

In his book, *The 21 Irrefutable Laws of Leadership*, John Maxwell discusses the "Law of Process" whereby "Champions don't become champions in the ring—they are merely recognized there."[2] In other words, when watching Michael Phelps win eight Olympic gold medals swimming in Beijing or Serena Williams winning her 4th Wimbledon title, all we see are the results, not the countless hours spent getting there through practice and training. These champions made a decision many years earlier that they wanted to become champions, and then did what they needed to do in order to achieve that level of success.

The Story of Kurt.

After a nice stint as an All-State high school quarterback in Cedar Rapids, Iowa, Kurt Warner was disappointed to learn that no Division I-A (FBS) college was willing to offer him a scholarship to play football. Shifting his focus, he accepted a partial scholarship to a smaller Division I-AA (FCS) school located about an hour's drive from home. Believing he would get to play early and often, he went to the University of Northern Iowa (UNI) where he would be relatively close to home and his family and friends could watch him play. He was wrong. After three long seasons riding the bench as a back-up quarterback, Warner finally won the starting position during his senior year. After a rocky start to the season, he ultimately earned Gateway Conference Offensive Player of the Year honors.

Warner believed that his level of play that year would be good enough to earn a spot in the NFL draft, but once again, he was wrong and went undrafted. However, in 1994 he was given a chance to earn a spot as a free agent on the roster of the Green Bay Packers, but he was competing against a young Brett Favre, veteran Mark Brunell and former Heisman Trophy winner Ty Detmer. He was cut from the team before the start of the season.

Shortly thereafter, Warner returned to Cedar Falls to work in a grocery store for $5.50 per hour stocking shelves and serve as a graduate assistant coach for his former UNI football team. With no NFL team willing to give him a tryout, Warner signed with the Iowa Barnstormers in 1995, part of the Arena Football League. He experienced great success in arena football and was named to the AFL's First-Team All-Arena in both 1996 and 1997 after leading the Barnstormers to the Arena Bowl (the league championship game) both seasons.

Because of his hard work and success with the Barnstormers, he signed in 1998 with the NFL St. Louis Rams and then subsequently was sent off to play for the NFL Europe Amsterdam Admirals, where he led the league in both touchdowns and passing yards. Following his season in Europe, he returned to the Rams and served as their third-string quarterback after beating out Will Furrer for the position.

At the beginning of the 1999 season, Warner became the second-string quarterback behind newly signed Trent Green. However, when Green tore his ACL in a preseason game, Warner finally was given his opportunity to take over the starting role. With the support of his coach, Dick Vermeil, and fellow teammates, Warner went on to have one of the best seasons in history for an NFL quarterback, throwing for over 4,300 yards, with 41 touchdown passes and a pass completion rate of over 65%. The Rams would go on to win Super Bowl XXXIV, and Warner would be named 1999 NFL Most Valuable Player as well as Super Bowl MVP, one of only seven players, including such NFL greats as Bart Starr, Joe Namath, Terry Bradshaw and Joe Montana, to receive both honors in the same year.[3,4]

Kurt Warner's journey to becoming a successful NFL quarterback demanded hard work and perseverance. He always knew what he wanted, but getting there wasn't easy. Unlike most NFL quarterbacks, who usually go through a simpler, more traditional process of career progression,

Warner's path was significantly longer and much more difficult; he had to humble himself and repeatedly accept "lesser" roles in football just to stay connected to the sport.

Despite all of his personal setbacks (that also included financial and family problems), he maintained a strong belief in his potential and did whatever he needed to do in order to achieve his goal of playing in the NFL. In his book, *All Things Possible*, Warner explains it this way:

> *I believe that the Lord has a plan for each of us that's better than anything we can imagine—even if that plan isn't obvious to us at every stage. He prepared me for this over a long period of time—in lower-profile locker rooms and the grocery store and in Europe, through all of the personal tragedies and in spite of the people who doubted me along the way...I realize now that I would not have been prepared for my big chance had it happened before it did.*[5]

My Experience.

Over the years, I've had the opportunity to teach a large number of college students in a variety of business-related topics. Most recently, my efforts have been with fourth-year students in a capstone strategy class designed to tie all of their prior business courses together with an applied focus.

One of the topics that I stress is the necessity of being willing to do whatever is needed in the short-term to ultimately achieve what is wanted over the long-term. Today's world has become extremely competitive; unfortunately, a college degree doesn't necessarily guarantee the job a person thinks he deserves just because he has one. As a result, a student may have to do something he really doesn't "want" to do in the early stages of his career, in order to position himself for that which he truly ***does*** want.

Most of my students somehow feel this principle doesn't apply to them, and ultimately, they will have to figure it out on their own. However, every now and then one of them will listen and take this advice to heart. In a recent email, Melissa, one of my former students, shared her job-seeking experience after she graduated:

> *Watching my friends graduate at a time when it's so hard to get a job, it saddens me to see the reactive state with which so many people have become comfortable. When they don't find their dream job within a couple of days searching, they attribute their difficulty to the economy and the horrors of the job market. It stuns me the lack of effort they put forth. I graduated with excellent grades and a degree in information systems. After graduating in May, I applied for jobs daily for months until I received my first interview at the end of August. I nailed the interview and landed my sweet gig...in reception.*
>
> *Never in a million years did I anticipate that all my hard work in school with a "legitimate" major would get me is a job that I could have just as easily received with a high school diploma. But I wanted a job, so I took it. With slightly bruised pride, I worked very hard to*

prove both my potential and desire to do bigger and better things. Ten months later, I was promoted into an entry level-job in my field of study...I was proactive, and finally felt as though I had direction in life.

The most astonishing thing to me is how all of my friends still complain almost a year later about being unemployed after graduation. Yet these are the very same people who turned down the opportunity to submit their resumes for my old reception position after my promotion because it was somehow beneath them.

Declining Drive.

As nearly any educator can attest, over the last couple of decades, students have changed. As a professor, beginning with my very first class, I have always given students the opportunity to write an extra-credit research paper should they decide to do so. The paper requirements and constraints are detailed in the course syllabus from the first day of class, and the paper is due the last day of class, thus giving students approximately four months to prepare it. The paper is worth up to an additional 10% of the final point total, so their final course grade could potentially improve by a full letter grade.

When I first began doing this, I would receive about 28 papers out of a class of 30 students, some from students who were already earning an "A" for the class. Today, in a class of 30 students, I'm doing well to receive five or six at most, or less than one-fourth of what I received twenty years ago (and the majority of these are turned in by students already earning an "A"). This change represents more than a 75% decline over two generations of students who are apparently unwilling to do "whatever they need to do" in order to guarantee a higher final course grade.

Over a span of five years, I also performed a non-scientific study with my fourth-year students in the strategy classes discussed earlier. During discussions of creative and innovative thinking, I had students break into groups of two and gave each group a bag containing a number of miscellaneous items, including some Lego® blocks, a penny, a nut, a bolt and a washer, a marble, wire nut, and a wooden spool. The task for each group was to divide all of the items into two distinct groups (i.e., things made of metal/ things not made of metal). They were to do this as many times as they could within 20 minutes. I also passed out a solution sheet for each two-person group that not only restated the instructions for the exercise—in boldface—but also included a number of lines so they could record their solutions. What I didn't tell them was that the number of solution lines per sheet gradually increased from 20 to 80 as the sheets were distributed across the room.

An interesting phenomenon occurred. Students completed the exercise and came up with as many solutions as possible ***up to*** the number of lines they were provided. In only one single instance (out of hundreds total) had a group gone beyond the number of provided lines. Although there were many fully completed sheets ranging from 20 to 80 solutions, typically once a group filled the respective number of lines, brainstorming stopped and the discussion shifted to just talking about random things while group members played around with the items. Although the instructions were clear and it was stressed that each group needed to come up with ***as many solutions as possible***, nearly all groups only worked up to the self-imposed, perceived limits of the exercise. Some groups arrived at 20 solutions, others 40, and still others 80, yet for the most part, students seemed equally content with the amount of effort they invested in the exercise (ironically, the list of solutions I have compiled over the years includes over a thousand possibilities).

These classroom examples provide anecdotal evidence as to how some students approach work today. I have also observed similar behavior patterns with many workers at all levels (e.g., not very willing to stay longer if the job isn't finished, only doing that which they are asked to do, and/or not taking much initiative outside of assigned tasks). These experiences, combined with similar stories shared by colleagues, lead me to believe there is a cultural pattern of a declining work ethic in comparison to what people ***say*** they want and desire.

It Keeps Going and Going and Going.

The concept of work ethic also implies a certain level of persistence. Sometimes getting what you want may require a bunch of extra time and effort doing what you need to do in order to get there, and persistent people know how to steer clear of vacuums. History is replete with examples of successful people who displayed extraordinarily high levels of perseverance and persistence to achieve their goals and dreams.

For example, James Dyson spent fifteen years and developed over 5100 prototypes to finally complete the design for his revolutionary vacuum cleaner (one that truly sucks compared to others in the market—pardon the pun). When no other manufacturer would take it on as part of an existing product line, Dyson launched Dyson Limited to manufacture and distribute it. Today, Dyson's vacuum generates the highest total sales revenue of any vacuum in the United States.[6]

Chester Carlson's idea for electrophotography was shot down more than twenty times by companies such as IBM and Kodak. Through his perseverance, however, he was able to finally enter into an agreement with a small photo-paper company called Haloid (later known as Xerox). Twenty-one years after initially inventing electrophotography (now known as xerography), the first convenient office copier using the technology was unveiled.[7] Imagine an office today without a photocopier or laser printer!

Dr. Seuss (a.k.a. Theodor Seuss Geisel) peddled his first children's book, *Mulberry Street*, to twenty-seven different publishers only to be rejected twenty-seven times. It wasn't until he literally bumped into an old college friend who happened to work at Vanguard Press, a division of Houghton Mifflin, that he was able to get his illustrations and manuscript in front of some key decision makers. Vanguard ultimately published the book which was well-received and jump-started a career that resulted in 44 children's books, nearly 30 of which have been adapted for television or video.[8]

Books, movies and television shows are loaded with examples of people like Dyson, Carlson, and Geisel (Dr.

Seuss). Why do we like these stories so much? Could it be that the people in these stories exhibit such a high degree of work ethic that one can only dream of reaching that level? Or could it be that most people believe that this kind of work ethic and persistence only exists in books or movies so the entire concept is fiction?

What If?

I remember the day my son purchased his first car, an old Chevy Cavalier with a ton of miles and a salvage title. Shortly after the purchase, he was in my driveway washing and waxing it. He even scrubbed the interior, washed the carpet and added a nice perfume scent. When I mentioned that I didn't ever recall him washing and waxing my car during all of the time he had driven it, he replied, "That car wasn't mine."

In reality, I believe most people share this same perspective. There's an old saying: "No one ever waxes a rental car." When there is little or no personal investment, it's really hard to place a lot of value on something. Sometimes we can see it in children and how they take care of their "free" stuff while growing up, college students who haven't made a personal financial investment into their education (or can't feel the pain of their student loans while still in school), and employees who are allowed to simply "exist" within a company and not pull their weight.

Unlike years past, we have a growing number of people who are receiving many of their "wants" without really having to make a personal investment into acquiring them.

This process of entitlement or guaranteed benefit leaves out the most important aspect of acquisition: the hard work associated with getting there. The process of creating personal value and self-esteem is why a strong work ethic is so important for the long-term growth of people. The resulting feelings of accomplishment, a goal achieved and personal success are what have driven this country and our entrepreneurial spirit since the beginning.

The role of leaders today at all levels—from parents to teachers to office managers to production supervisors to the President of the United States—should be to facilitate an environment of self-growth, to support the efforts of other people, and to provide help and inspirational guidance along the way. The more success people have "doing whatever they need to do in order to get whatever they want," the more they will be driven to repeat the process another time while also helping others get what they want. Their sense of self-esteem and value will drive their personal growth and encourage them to reach higher levels of success. Their passion for work will become contagious and spread to others around them.

Someone once said, "There are no menial jobs, only menial attitudes." In his book *Brain Droppings*, comedian George Carlin observes, "Most people work just hard enough not to get fired and get paid just enough money not to quit."[9]

Imagine.

What if people suddenly realized there is honor in all work? What if they saw the value of hard work as a way to give?

What if everyone in your family, company or organization had a stronger work ethic? What if they all worked just a little bit harder, and their noses moved a little closer to the grindstone? What if?

Fighting Off the Purple People Eaters

- [ ] Stop trying to multitask your way through life. Focus on one thing at a time, put all of your energy into it, and get it done!

- [ ] Feel like you're on the sidelines suffering from "spectatoritis"? Get in the game and do something that helps you fire-up a little passion. People "buy" feelings, and passion gains support for ideas.

- [ ] What do you do well? Do it. What do you enjoy doing most? Do it. If they are not the same thing, then find a way to merge the two, and like Nike®, "Just Do It."

CHAPTER 6

Big Leaps & Baby Steps.

If you start to take Vienna–then take Vienna.

– Napoleon

It's the Thought That Counts.

I was once asked to teach a college capstone marketing class for two semesters for a professor on sabbatical. The students were fourth-year marketing majors, and the purpose of the class was to bring their marketing education together into a holistic, strategic context.

To provide them with "real world" marketing experience, I arranged to collaborate with a local business that manufactured and sold a high-end product line. The owner of the business agreed to let teams of five students each develop strategic marketing plans and create promotional campaigns for his business (which was especially appropriate since college-aged students are one of the primary target audiences of his product line).

The culmination of the project was a formal presentation made by each team before a panel of judges, which consisted of the company owner, two experienced local marketing professionals, and me. The owner promised to use all or part of the winning team's approach to market the company's product and agreed to give each student of the winning team a $250 Visa® gift card. Thus students had both financial and résumé-boosting incentives to perform well. The owner also agreed to cover any out-of-pocket presentation expenses up to $100 per team.

As the judges listened to the presentations that first semester, it quickly became apparent the students lacked passion and motivation for the project. Members of the panel frequently commented about how difficult it was to select a winning approach. In general, the projects lacked creativity; some ideas seemed to be little more than knock-offs of existing approaches (or tired, old ones). It was clear the majority of students hadn't invested enough time on the projects or the presentations (some which bordered on being unprofessional).

After some convincing (and a little pleading) on my part, the owner agreed to sponsor the project again the second semester. This time, I was determined to not make any assumptions regarding the skills of college students who were about to graduate and to provide them with the tools necessary to be successful.

I devoted several class sessions to the concepts of strategic creativity, professional presentation, influence and risk-taking. Instead of merely assuming that students were frequently meeting outside of class to work on their projects (as the little time I had provided in class that first semester didn't seem to be well utilized), I set aside a greater amount of class time for them to work on their projects (despite the fact the physical classroom space really wasn't conducive to groups working simultaneously). I actively engaged the groups and served as a resource throughout this time.

The end result: an outcome worse than the first. Not only were the presentations even more disappointing, the panel members became concerned about the overall quality of potential marketing graduates of the institution. My excitement and anticipation of providing students with a great professional opportunity quickly shifted to embarrassment. Even worse, my views of today's college graduates had been negatively altered in a significant way.

So What's the Problem?

Initially, I believed the problem rested squarely with the students: they lacked the motivation, work ethic and creativity required to be successful. What student wouldn't want to earn some cash and gain additional résumé experience right before venturing into the world of job hunting? But, after some soul-searching, I realized that some of the problem resided with me. Perhaps I had made too many assumptions; perhaps I didn't create an inspiring environment for learning to take place. Naively, I had simply assumed what appealed to me would also appeal to them. In short, I failed to be an effective leader in the classroom.

Please don't misunderstand. I still believe the students didn't exhibit the necessary motivation, work ethic and creativity to be successful. However, I have also come to realize—and better understand—my responsibility as the leader of the class to create an environment that increases the likelihood of those traits occurring. Unfortunately for all involved, it took two semesters and a bunch of wasted time and money for me to reach that level of understanding.

Motivation and the Influence of Environment.

Research in the field of psychology indicates that desired human behavior (or action) is a function of motivation, ability and opportunity. While the level of motivation determines the degree of attempt, ability and opportunity will determine whether the behavior can be successfully exhibited.[1] A leader can have the greatest impact by creating an environment that influences individual perceptions of both ability and opportunity. By reinforcing what people already know and tying that knowledge to available opportunities, leaders will have greater success in mobilizing desired behaviors as long as the necessary internal motivation to act is present.

My students could have been motivated in a variety of ways, of course, ranging from a genuine interest to learn to simply enduring the process in order to obtain the necessary credits to graduate. At the time, I didn't ask (at least conceptually) whether they would rather enjoy or endure the class, nor did I create an environment around the exercise that was dynamic and engaging regardless of what motivated them, one where students believed they had the necessary prior knowledge or one where students could see the project's long-term value. Although the opportunity for learning was present, not all students *recognized* the opportunity. Combine this lack of recognition with the team aspect of the project, where varying levels of perception and motivation must come together, and the result is a recipe for an unproductive project environment and lackluster student performance.

Because of this experience, I now evaluate behavioral outcomes within a broader environmental context, one which includes both psychological and spatial elements. For example, think about a typical elementary classroom with its walls totally covered with student work, learning tools, visuals, and positive, colorful images. What would happen to this environment if these were all suddenly removed? What would it do to the energy in the room? How would it affect student feelings and motivation? For whatever reason, most classrooms in higher educational institutions are just like this—empty and void of positive influences. The same can also be said of a great many production floors, offices and workspaces. To maximize outcomes as a leader, I must continuously assess the work environment in relation to assigned tasks to be completed by doers at all levels.

The Big Three.

Leadership, though, requires more than just an understanding of environment. Many other intangible aspects of leadership will directly influence the ultimate behavior of others. A quick perusal of the leadership section at Barnes & Noble® or a search on Amazon® (which yielded over 75,000 resources on leadership the last time I looked) can supply a nearly unlimited supply of advice. However, my experience suggests three core leadership principles, that when applied regularly over time, have helped me connect with people and impact their level of motivation: ***Get Behind and Push***, ***Walk the Talk***, and ***Think Big, Execute Small***.

Get Behind and Push.

Successful leaders must first be successful followers. Only leaders who know how to take direction, acknowledge responsibility, and accept accountability for their actions can truly understand leadership and its impact. I learned this very early in life. When I was a child, it was still socially acceptable for a child to receive a spanking whenever "exhibiting" some unacceptable behavior. Fortunately, in my case the spankings administered by my parents hurt just enough to remind me that my behavior was not acceptable and would not be tolerated. My parents weren't at all physically or mentally abusive; however, their actions played a large part in teaching me how to follow directions and gain the understanding that I would be held responsible and accountable for my actions.

Along with being a successful follower, a real leader also knows it's the doers that get the job done. So point the direction (preferably one that's a big leap) and get out the way while supporting the process. Strong leaders push others toward success. They recognize that when their people are successful, they too are successful, and success is mutual. In his book, *You Don't Know Me from Adam*, Adam Carroll discusses how real leaders activate the law of reciprocity: when you help enough other people achieve their goals, your own goals cannot help but be met. Put simply, givers get. Succeeding faster only requires one thing: a selfless devotion to helping other people achieve success by assisting them with contacts, resources, information and guidance.[2]

This system of support also includes understanding and connecting to others by caring and being interested, by acknowledging and sharing in their ups and downs, by treating them fairly and as equally important, and by viewing them as partners instead of subordinates. Strong leaders create an almost "family-like" supportive environment where relationships are necessary, trust is built, and it's in everyone's long-term interest to help others succeed. They never put themselves in a position to take something of value from those they are leading, which would ultimately devalue effort and kill motivation.

Walk the Talk.

Leadership is a daily process, not a destination. Before you can effectively lead others, you must be first able to lead yourself. In other words, a strong leader leads by example and knows that personal character will set the tone for everyone else. You must consistently display the character traits required by everyone to ensure success. Dependability, patience, self-discipline, integrity, confidence and a strong work ethic become daily expectations of you. Others cannot be expected to do that which you are unwilling to do, and a good leader knows that a consistent, high level of character is critical, whether one "feels" like it every day or not. Character can't be faked. One's character is reflected when no one is watching, and others will see through insincerity.

Not only should effective leaders set the bar of expectation, they should try to do "a little bit more" and consistently meet and exceed these expectations each and every time. Most people tend to value how others make them feel and will attempt to acquire the feelings they desire by associating themselves with those who exhibit them. (We like to be around others who make us feel better about ourselves.) By accepting a leadership role, you commit to a higher standard, one that not only requires a strong character but also demands a positive attitude.

A story of two bricklayers illustrates this concept. One day, a pedestrian stopped to admire the skill of two men who were laying bricks. She asked the first bricklayer, "What are you making?" In a somewhat gruff voice, the bricklayer responded, "About $15.50 an hour." At a loss for words, the pedestrian stepped over to the next bricklayer and asked, "Say, what are you making?" The second bricklayer happily replied, "I'm making the greatest cathedral in the world!"[3] Same activity, same question, two totally different responses. A positive attitude will change one's total perspective of something. A good leader chooses to see problems as opportunities to do great things versus mere labor.

If you have ever ridden a rollercoaster, you know that a wide variety of attitudes can be exhibited on any given ride. Some close their eyes, hold on for dear life, and can't wait for the ride to be over, while others ride with eyes wide open, arms outstretched, and love every second. Same ride, two entirely different emotional responses, but those in the latter group typically take the lead by sitting up front.

Attitude is a game changer. It often reflects the tone of leadership and dictates the response to failure. Babe Ruth had to strike out 1,330 times in order to hit 714 home runs (both once records in professional baseball) and lead the Yankees® to multiple championships;[4] Walt Disney was fired from his newspaper job for a lack of creative ideas;[5] Thomas Edison (who held over 1000 patents for his inventions) was pulled out of school as a child after his schoolmaster called him "addle-minded" and "slow;"[6] Michael Jordan missed over 9000 shots in his career, lost 300 games, and missed 26 final game-winning shots on his way leading the Bulls® to six NBA championships;[7] and Lee Iacocca, having been fired from Ford® after 32 years of service, went on to lead Chrysler® back to success after the company was on the brink of bankruptcy.[8]

Attitude is an outward expression of the heart. If you truly want others to be successful, then maintaining a consistent positive attitude is paramount. People can easily become discouraged by any one of a large number of aspects in their lives. A positive attitude by those in charge—as well as a positive environment—can help them overcome those feelings and develop a renewed sense of energy. Strong leaders strive to exhibit a positive attitude every day in order to help others exhibit one on most days.

Think Big, Execute Small.

Some people today tend to view the primary role of leadership as having and setting long-term vision (determining a direction) while letting others figure out how to get there. However, effective leaders are not only able to visualize which mountain to climb but also the individual steps necessary to climb it.

In the 1991 comedy *What About Bob?* Bill Murray plays Bob Wiley, a character suffering from some serious "issues" (the clinical diagnosis given in the movie was "an extreme case of multi-phobic personality characterized by acute separation anxiety"). When Bob's current psychologist pawns him off on Dr. Leo Marvin, an egotistical psychologist played by Richard Dreyfuss, Bob shows up at Dr. Marvin's office for an initial interview. As Dr. Marvin is getting ready to leave on vacation for a month, he shoves a copy of his new book, *Baby Steps*, into Bob's hands and sends him on his way. The premise of the book is to help people achieve larger goals by visualizing much smaller, reasonable goals and then take a series of successive baby steps to get there. To the eventual dismay of Dr. Marvin, Bob totally takes the doctor's words to heart. He is able to visualize and take each necessary, yet very difficult, step towards "sharing" Dr. Marvin's vacation with his family. Bob's actions include walking to the bus terminal, getting on the bus, riding the bus to Camp Winnipesaukee in New Hampshire, finding Dr. Marvin by yelling for him in the middle of town, and then hijacking Dr. Marvin's book interview with *Good Morning America*. Bob humorously "baby steps" his way into every aspect of Dr. Marvin's life and ultimate psychotic breakdown.[9]

Although they desire a different outcome, strong leaders are like Bob. They are able to "see" a big leap, some potential great outcome or challenging opportunity, and then visualize and implement each baby step necessary to achieve it. With laser-like focus, they accomplish each required step in sequence while keeping the big picture and ultimate outcome in mind the entire time. They realize that 20% of their effort accounts for 80% of their success (Pareto's Principle) so they don't allow themselves to be overcome by vaccums and irrelevant daily minutia. Able to manage many steps simultaneously while keeping the appropriate priority on each, leaders also recognize forward progress is a process. They are patient; sometimes great things may take considerable time to accomplish. In the Old Testament of the Bible, King Solomon says, "It is better to finish something than to start it. It is better to be patient than to be proud."[10]

Strong leaders will assemble great teams of doers who are able to execute. They will find, and nurture, those who can work both individually and collaboratively. They know that individual effort impacts the outcome of the entire group, so leaders are willing to work with doers to improve individual performance. Effective leaders are also willing to reorganize tasks and people to gain maximum output or remove some people altogether if necessary.

Imagine a snow globe. As long as each snowflake continues to fall, the desired effect is achieved. Sometimes, however, after the "snow" settles, the globe needs a good shake to reenergize it and keep things moving. Strong leaders are snow globe shakers. Have you shaken yours recently?

Fighting Off the Purple People Eaters

- ☐ Aspire to be better—not the best. The "best" comes and goes, often replaced by another. If you are trying to simply improve a little each time regardless of what you are doing, the rest will come.

- ☐ Support others. They will return the favor.

- ☐ List five areas/things where you typically procrastinate. What is it about them that you don't like doing?

- ☐ List five things that you enjoy doing. What is it about them that you enjoy? Set goals that include more of these things and less of the others above.

CHAPTER 7

Remember the Alamoon!

That's one small step for man; one giant leap for mankind.

– Neil A. Armstrong, Commander, Apollo 11 & First Man to Walk on the Moon

Whoopie! Man, that may have been a small one for Neil, but it's a long one for me.

– Charles "Pete" Conrad, Jr., Commander, Apollo 12 & Third Man to Walk on the Moon (and the shortest Apollo astronaut).

July 20, 1969.

I will never forget July 20, 1969. I was visiting my grandmother, sitting in front of her black and white television, watching CBS News anchor Walter Cronkite shed a tear as Neil Armstrong placed his boot on the moon for the first time. As a young child, I had no real concept of the significance of the event. I just thought it was cool he was on the moon.

However "cool" it may have been to watch, that single event inspired an entire generation—my generation. It showed us that we could do almost anything if we worked hard enough and put our minds to it. It served as the driving force behind much of what we accomplished for the next few decades. Whenever a project or business activity reached a stumbling point or hurdle, the common phrase became "What, we can put a man on the moon, but we can't…?" It's also what personally motivated me to excel in school and focus on math, science and electronics. In fact, as a high school kid in the late 1970s, I was developing personal computers and dabbling in robotics, both of which earned me a spot in the International Science and Engineering Fair, all because of the inspiration I received from the Apollo program and the astronauts who served as my personal rock stars. (Ok, so I was a bit of a nerd.)

Flash forward to March 5, 2010. The college where I serve as provost hosted its first annual Celebrate! Innovation Week (ciWeek 2010). The theme for the week was the Apollo Moon missions, and our keynote speaker for the event was Captain Alan Bean, Apollo 12 and Skylab III astronaut and the fourth man to walk on the moon.

I chose the Apollo program as the theme for our first Celebrate! Innovation Week because it serves as one of the greatest examples of innovative thinking and problem solving in the history of mankind. Those involved in the program had a very short period of time (less than nine years) to meet the deadline given by President John F. Kennedy in a speech to a joint session of Congress. Those involved had to invent over 80% of the technology required, and successful completion of the program required the participation of over 400,000 people and 10,000 organizations and companies—a massive project to say the least.

The result was the development of the Saturn V—a rocket that towered 363 feet, weighed about 6.7 million pounds, and featured over 2 million functioning parts, all controlled by a computer with less power than what can be found in today's smartphones. The entire rocket package enabled three astronauts to travel a quarter of a million miles to the moon, a heavenly body that is in constant motion in relationship to the earth. And the entire feat was accomplished by using the power of the human mind (the Internet, the personal computer and even calculators didn't yet exist).[1]

Alan Bean's speech during ciWeek was inspiring as he detailed the events leading up to the successful completion of President Kennedy's vision. However, there was a repeated theme throughout his presentation about the lack of knowledge and understanding necessary to get someone to the moon and how it required a large group of smart, but very average people working together to accomplish the mission. Since it hadn't been done before, no one knew exactly what to do, so they had to learn how to communicate effectively, solve problems as a team, manage large-scale projects, and most importantly maintain their drive and passion during failures and setbacks. To illustrate the "work-in-progress" and "learn-as-we-go" approach to the project, NASA stated in 1962 that the Apollo launch vehicle would be a "white-and-silver shaft jutting majestically 185 feet into the still-cool morning air." This statement only underestimated the eventual design by about 200 feet.[2]

During our time together, I found Captain Bean to be warm, friendly, intelligent and talented, but he was also the very type of person he talked about during his speeches, an average person (just like you and me) who had to figure things out on the fly while working with other people to accomplish something beyond what had been only imagined previously. Whether listening to his formal ciWeek presentations or just casually talking while eating a burger at lunch, Captain Bean inspired me to reexamine my ideas about the roles of both leaders and followers.

Where Should the Focus Be?

I don't believe that anyone today can dispute that we tend to put our leaders on pedestals and praise them for their greatness in overseeing a successful accomplishment. Whether it's Steve Jobs, Martin Luther King, Mother Teresa, Vince Lombardi, General Dwight D. Eisenhower, or George Washington, we have always admired leaders for the great outcomes that occur under their leadership. We buy the many books either written by them or about them, we complete studies to determine common characteristics they share, and business colleges and others spend countless hours analyzing them. However, after listening to Captain Bean and thinking about the larger picture of process, I think that our focus has sometimes been misdirected.

I am not trying to downplay the importance of strong leadership. It takes a leader to set forth vision and direction and to accept responsibility and be accountable. It takes a leader to build a team capable of getting the job done. And it takes a leader to serve as a unifying force during the entire process. Without President Kennedy's vision, we might never have gone to the moon. Even after his death, he still served as a unifying force for those working on Apollo to remain steadfast during a difficult time in this country.

However, after thinking about the process as a whole, I believe we need to refocus our emphasis. We should be spending much more time focusing on the people who get the job done: the people who do everything necessary to actually achieve the vision set forth by the leader. These people, the "doers" for lack of a better term, are those who apply their education and skills to design and build the parts, the soldiers who put their lives on the line storming the beaches of foreign countries, the players who spend six days a week training hard for a three-hour game on Sunday, and the staffers who regularly work overtime to make sure reports are submitted by deadline. In the words of Alan Bean, these are the "average people who come together to do something great."

Without the doers, nothing would actually ever be accomplished. Therefore, the doers should be receiving far more of the credit and accolades for achieving the outcomes set forth by leaders. These doers made going to moon possible, they won the battles at Omaha Beach (D-Day) and Iwo Jima during WWII, they play and win the Super Bowl, and they get the presentation finished on time for the big meeting with the prospective client. The world needs doers…lots of them. Without them, nothing happens.

Doers Can Also Inspire.

In 1836, Mexican General Santa Anna marched his army of more than 1500 soldiers against the approximately 200 Texian soldiers defending the Alamo Mission. On their third advance, Santa Anna's army overwhelmed the Texians (later known as Texans after Texas joined the Union). They were either brutally slain or executed in the process and only the noncombatants were spared to share the story of the defeat with hopes of putting the fear of the Mexican Army in other Texians. However, the opposite occurred, and men flocked to join the Texian Army commanded by General Sam Houston. The rallying cry of "Remember the Alamo!" became the central motivator of the revived Texian Army which went on to quickly defeat the Mexican Army and secure the independence of the Republic of Texas.

Although the doers at the Alamo (the soldiers and volunteers) were outnumbered 7 to 1 and most certainly knew they would not survive repeated attacks by the Mexican Army, they demonstrated that with the right focus, a group of average people can do something extraordinary. Not only were they able to take out about a third of the Mexican Army during the battles, their sacrifice at the Alamo unified and inspired what was then a fragmented and disorganized Texian Army.[3]

What Makes a Good Doer Today?

We need many people to accept the roles of doers: we need those who are task intelligent and capable, united towards a common goal, willing to go above and beyond when needed, able to formulate and ask questions to understand and develop clarity of thought, open to necessary change, and willing to follow others. The process requires a coordinated effort on the part of doers who can effectively communicate and work as a team.

When Vince Lombardi was the coach of the Green Bay Packers, they relied heavily on a play known as the "Power Sweep." The play required players to pull out of their normal positions in order to block downfield while the running back would run to wherever the other team wasn't. It wasn't a trick play or something very glitzy, but it was a very effective play that allowed the Packers to win five NFL championships. Lombardi once said, "It's my number one play because it requires all eleven men to play as one to make it succeed, and that's what 'team' means."[4]

The Power of One.

Ultimately, success comes down to the individual, regardless of the size of organization, group or team. It's been said that a single person can change the world, but a single person can also derail an entire process. A single player out of position can quickly cause even a simple play to fail.

Although it's the role of leaders to focus on what the big puzzle will look like, it's the role of doers to focus on putting their specific pieces in place. If all doers are maximizing their personal effectiveness, then the puzzle will successfully come together. For doers to be effective in their respective roles, they must understand the importance of proactive personal leadership and its direct impact on the five areas of personal health: ***physical, emotional, intellectual, spiritual,*** and ***financial***.

Physical Health: Directly Impacts Energy Level

Numerous studies point to the relationship between physical health and productivity. Feeling good results in less down time, a better attitude, and more energy. There are many reasons why a growing number of companies are instituting wellness programs (with lower heath care costs being not the least of them). Physical health requires a life consisting of a controlled calorie diet and exercise and the personal discipline to fight off the constant barrage of vacuums that try to distract all of us from achieving our goals.

Emotional Health: Affects the Quality of Life and Work

Numerous studies have also shown a direct relationship between physical health and emotional state (and vice versa). Stress, burnout, alcohol and drug abuse, depression and a wide variety of other mental health concerns have a direct impact on productivity and serve as distractions to effective outcomes. Engaging in positive activities and doing the things you enjoy will help you feel better about yourself and maintain a sense of balance in life.

Intellectual Health: Continues Throughout Life

Lifelong learning is a must, especially with life's rapid changes today. Reading, taking additional classes, attending workshops and seminars, watching certain programming on television, and sometimes even playing games will not only improve your intellectual and problem-solving abilities, they can also be fun and relaxing, thereby improving both emotional and physical health.

Spiritual Health: Creates Purpose and Virtue

Believing in something greater gives purpose and direction to life. It creates the values, principles, and virtues that form the foundation for the decisions you make and directions you take throughout life. Realizing that there's more to life than just you illuminates how your piece fits within life's big puzzle. It makes you a more effective member of your family, your team at work, and your community. For example, a thorough reading of our Declaration of Independence, Constitution, and Bill of Rights (all written by our founding fathers) displays a strong spiritual influence and belief in God.

Financial Health: Allows Sustainable Choices

As evidenced by the relentless commercials for credit counselors and recent legal changes in order to "crack down on credit card company practices," many people today face ever-increasing debt and the physical and emotional stress which results. Those who are financially healthy know how to live within their means (thus requiring a budget) and work hard to both eliminate and stay out of debt.

Obviously, all of these areas are closely related and work hand-in-hand. Personal leadership is a holistic process that continually addresses all five areas of personal health simultaneously. The key to personal leadership is that it is proactive. You have to decide to be healthy. You have to take action towards having a better state of health. You have to follow through on that action. And you have to evaluate the outcomes as you go and adjust as necessary. It's all about doing something to create active change, and not just hoping for a different outcome.

Of all the words and catch-phrases popular today, the one I personally dislike the most is the misuse of the word "hope." Hope is not a strategy. It's not a vision or plan. It's not proactive or action-oriented. And it's definitely not about effort or actually applying yourself. People "hope" for things to improve their lives. They "hope" for positive changes, and they "hope" that things will just come their way or perhaps that others will fix their problems. In reality, I believe that hope—without a clear understanding of the larger effort needed—can serve as an excuse to do nothing at all, or at the very least, to avoid the discipline and persistence required to accomplish anything of real substance. If we had just "hoped" to get to the moon, it would have never happened.

I recognize that hope might be all that's possible for things outside our control. We hope that a giant meteor doesn't crash into and destroy the Earth, and we hope that cars won't cross over the centerline and hit us head on. But hope alone is often inadequate for things within our control. In this regard, hope actually can become a paralyzing force if people simply wait on the actions of others or outside events to occur.

The people who have demonstrated great leadership over their lives and in the lives of others don't "hope," they "do." They are doers. They are the people who are willing to do their part and not simply wait on others to do theirs. They are willing to do the jobs (or tasks) that no one else really wants to do, and then do them with a positive attitude.

When I was young, my parents would repeatedly stress, "If you are going to do something, then do your best, or don't do it at all." Sometimes I wonder if we are moving towards a "I'd rather not do it at all" mode of living. Based on personal observation, if parents are still teaching this vital lesson to their children, then for some it must be going "in one ear and out the other" (something else my father would often say).

I once had the honor of visiting the National World War II Museum in New Orleans. One thing that I took away from this moving experience more than anything else was the overwhelming sense of sacrifice on the part of everyone for the greater good of the country. Everyone—leaders, doers, ordinary citizens, those in combat and those who were not—helped to fight Hitler's Nazis and the Japanese Empire. Everyone played an important role, whether it was fighting in battles, working in factories, or rationing and conserving resources. People knew that if they personally came up short, it could negatively affect the entire outcome. Personal leadership and discipline were the norm.

The same was true during the Apollo program in the 1960s. It's been reported many times that early in the program during a tour of one of NASA's facilities, John F. Kennedy asked a janitor who was sweeping the floors what he did for NASA. He replied, "I'm putting a man on the moon." Although the specifics of this story seem to vary, thus putting the factual nature of the account in question, my conversations with Alan Bean confirmed that this very attitude exhibited the essence of NASA during the Apollo program. He said, "Everyone knew their role and its importance towards accomplishing the goal. A group of average people were able to work together, each doing their part, to achieve something great."

Whether it's the legacy of the battle at the Alamo, the sacrifices made during World War II, or the motivated efforts of over 400,000 people in the Apollo program, history is loaded with positive examples of personal leadership and the necessary commitment demonstrated by all to accomplish shared goals. As we face growing challenges as a country, as companies, and as individuals, history needs to happen now. Hope isn't working, and personal leadership, responsibility and accountability should be placed front and center. People must recognize the importance and influence of their small piece of the larger puzzle and stop bemoaning the inadequacies of others. If everyone does their part, regardless of the context, then every puzzle will come together in some manner. And perhaps to get there, we should all take on a new rallying cry, "Remember the Alamoon!"

- ☐ When do you use words like "hope," "wish," or "if only" when discussing goals? How passionate are you about accomplishing them? Do you believe you can? If not, then you won't. Find ways to make progress, even slightly, towards your goals. Success begets motivation which begets more success.

- ☐ Are your words and actions consistent with your goals? They should be in harmony with each other. How can you correct your negative self-talk? Change your words.

- ☐ Have you shared your goals with those closest to you or with your "sounding board"? If not, do it. You will need buy-in from those you respect to create a supportive environment, which will enhance your chances of success.

CHAPTER 8

Cows Aren't Always Cows.

Be yourself; everyone else is already taken.

– Oscar Wilde

An Image Perception Story.

Back in my early days of college, I worked as an assistant manager in a 24-hour grocery store. Being the lowest link on the managerial food chain, I was given the joyous responsibility to oversee the ever-popular 11 p.m. to 7 a.m. time slot (a shift which allowed me the opportunity to observe some incredibly interesting, sometimes disturbing people). During these hours, customer traffic would be typically slow, so we used the time to clean, stock and face merchandise, build product displays, and sometimes just goof off.

One of my last responsibilities each morning was to check in the daily milk delivery. One day, for whatever reason, it dawned on me that ALL of our milk, regardless of brand, came off of the same truck. (At the time I wasn't privy to the more than $100,000 I have since spent on higher education and didn't yet fully understand the concepts of private labeling and multi-branding.) At the time, though, I thought it was a brilliant and astute observation.

Our store carried three distinct "brands" of milk: Borden® (the primary national brand with "Elsie the Cow" as its mascot), Parade® (our store brand), and generic (boring white label with black text only). All of these brands came in a variety of flavors and types including whole, 2%, 1% and skim.

Since it seemed unusual at the time that the same truck would deliver all of our milk, I felt compelled to ask the driver if he had to make several separate dairy stops in order to get it all. His response actually surprised me. "No," he said, "they all come from the same dairy; cows are cows."

He was right. There were no such things as Borden cows (although "Elsie" made a strong visual case otherwise), Parade cows, or "generic" cows. The delivery driver went on to explain that the same exact milk is in each container, only the labels were different.

Cows are Cows, and Milk is Milk.

I then went on a mission (or a crusade if you will). I tried to actually "help" people by pointing out there was really no difference between the three brands. (My bosses didn't mind since we actually made higher margins on the cheaper milk.) I distinctly remember a particular instance when I tried to explain this to an elderly lady who appeared to be on a fixed budget (remember what happens when you "ass-u-me").

When I saw her reach for the Borden milk, I quickly, but politely, suggested there was absolutely no difference between the brands and that she could actually save money by purchasing the generic instead. I received a look I will never forget, one that suggested I was a combination of ignorant, stupid, and naïve, at best. She then proceeded to inform me that she had been drinking milk for about four times as long as I had been alive and that I should basically mind my own business.

This was my first real lesson in branding and image: ***Perceptions of reality are more important than reality itself, and it is perceptions that drive people and behavior.***

Despite having the exact same content, the packaging of the products created perceptions that were subsequently extended to the content itself. Elsie was a cartoon cow that had a very sweet and soft feminine voice in the Borden commercials. The consumer couldn't help but like Elsie, and her support of Borden milk added value to the product related to the perception of quality. It didn't matter that she was a cartoon. In the mind of the consumer she represented the ideals of being pure and wholesome. The Parade brand was only as good as the consumer's views of the store itself. As long as the consumer trusted the store, the consumer more than likely trusted its store-labeled products (although not to the same degree as beloved Elsie). As for the "generic" brand with its simple black text on a plain white background: despite no difference in product quality, why would anyone trust this product when given the choice? How good could it really be when no one was willing to put a name on it?

However, regardless of someone's current perception, it only takes one event, one issue, or one bad accusation to totally change how something is viewed. What if you found out (or even if someone simply made the accusation) that the cows that produced a particular brand's milk were being drugged, abused or painfully electro-shocked in order to produce higher quantities of milk? I doubt any cartoon cow in the world would be able to overcome that. What if it was reported that one of the store-labeled cans of beans had a dead mouse in it? Even if the store-labeled milk came from a completely different supplier than the beans, I'll bet that this would affect most people's view of all of the store-branded products. And as for the "generic," enough said.

Image is a lot like trust. You spend a lifetime building it and all it takes is one negative moment to tear down a lifetime's worth of effort. This is also true when it comes to your personal image. It's not just milk producers or even cola and shoe companies that have to be concerned about image. Whether you are a business professional, politician, athlete, parent, student, or just someone trying to get by and make ends meet, your personal image is more important now than ever before. It can change in an instant, often before you even know it. I realize that the concept of "personal image" may seem somewhat cheesy or unseemly to some people. But unlike past generations, where news traveled slowly and reputation was often formed by direct interactions with a few relatively local people, technology has changed all that. The sheer speed and ease by which information is disseminated has become a game-changer.

Because people now tend to live at least part, if not most of their lives online through Facebook®, LinkedIn®, Twitter®, FourSquare®, Flickr®, YouTube®, blogs, and a variety of other sites (including some, like my personal website, which may even seem "old-fashioned" by young audiences), a huge amount of online content has been created and shared, with or without permission. This content will tell people more about you than ever before: who you are, what you do, and why you matter. Whether you like it or not, this image is being formed by the daily interactions you have with almost anyone, regardless of how formal the relationship. Although reputation historically developed over time, it can now be shaped immediately, and search engines (like Google®) have made it nearly impossible to "hide" from anything, good or bad. In today's world, your personal image is the most important asset you own, and it will directly affect both how people perceive you and your success in most aspects of your life, whether their perception is shaped by your relationships with others, your job, or even your credit score. Leaders of all types and at all levels must have a positive personal image to effectively influence others. If you take personal leadership seriously, then you must do the same when it comes to your personal image.

So How is Image Created?

Others' perception of you is influenced by what they think about you, including how they look at you, how they feel when doing it, what they see, how they mentally categorize you in terms of others, and how (or if) they personally identify with you. In essence, your image (despite what you personally may believe it to be) is closely aligned to your reputation, which is interpreted by a variety of different people whose moods, perspectives, perceptions, attitudes, values, and feelings vary between them.

Although a great many "brand experts" will state that you can proactively create your personal image and how people "see" you, I personally believe that ultimately you are who you are, regardless of how you may present yourself to others. Although you may be able to fake being "someone else" for a little while, others will soon see through your charade, especially with the advent of rapidly changing technologies. Your personal image today is now closely tied with your personal identity and ultimately all things you. No one can really hide from technology today, so it's actually in your best interest to be transparent and authentic. (In other words, be who you are and stop trying to be someone else.)

In the movie *The Devil Wears Prada*, Miranda Priestly, the harsh fashion "devil" in the movie played by Meryl Streep, makes an enlightening statement as she attempts to educate her new underling about the "stuff" of fashion:

> *This...stuff? Oh. Okay. I see. You think this has nothing to do with you. You go to your closet and you select...I don't know...that lumpy blue sweater, for instance because you're trying to tell the world that you take yourself too seriously to care about what you put on your back. But what you don't know is that sweater is not just blue, it's not turquoise. It's not lapis. It's actually cerulean. And you're*

also blithely unaware of the fact that in 2002, Oscar de la Renta did a collection of cerulean gowns. And then I think it was Yves Saint Laurent...wasn't it who showed cerulean military jackets?...And then cerulean quickly showed up in the collections of eight different designers. And then it filtered down through the department stores and then trickled on down into some tragic Casual Corner where you, no doubt, fished it out of some clearance bin. However, that blue represents millions of dollars and countless jobs and it's sort of comical how you think that you've made a choice that exempts you from the fashion industry when, in fact, you're wearing the sweater that was selected for you by the people in this room from a pile of stuff. [1]

In a world driven by psychological shaping through the power of what "they" say ("they" being the product brands, celebrities, athletes, media, and just about anyone else who attempts to influence us today), the importance of being genuine has never been greater.

Meet Your Digital Personality.

Through ever-improving search engines, it has become nearly impossible to separate our lives into distinct categories, such as personal and professional. Your life is now seen by others to be one large clump of all things you, a holistic "digital personality" so to speak, and everyone has one (on the flipside, not showing up in web searches also says something about you). As a result, everything in your life now ultimately affects everything else which can and will directly affect your future.

Since your digital personality represents all things online related to you, something as simple and innocent as a post to someone's blog, a post on Facebook, or an uploaded photo or YouTube video (or being "tagged" by someone else) can have permanent consequences. For example, as a college professor, I know of at least two specific cases in which straight "A" students were denied jobs because of some questionable aspects of their digital personalities. Unlike generations past, the choices we make today have a tendency to stick with us, possibly forever. At the rapidly growing rate of "online spread" (a term I use to describe the exponential spread of content and information through online reposting and tagging), even a few negative words about you (true or otherwise) can have disastrous effects.

This cultural shift in information transmission is also not a "generational thing" only relegated to young people. Although many areas of the Internet are still dominated by the "millennial" generation, older generations (Gen Xers and Boomers) have made huge gains. According to information found in the "Internet & American Life Project" of the PEW Research Center, the fastest growth in social network sites has come from older Internet users. Blogging has shown greater gains with the older generations, and older users are more likely to engage simultaneously in several different online activities (such as research, reading the news, visiting social sites, responding to email, and watching videos).[2]

Even an "old-school" capitalist like Warren Buffet, CEO of Berkshire Hathaway, knows the importance of image and reputation. Buffet was quoted in a *New York Times* article in regards to the dismissal of David Sokol (once seen as his potential successor), "We can afford to lose money–even a lot of money. But we can't afford to lose reputation–even a shred of reputation."[3] If Warren Buffet is willing to lose substantial money rather than a shred of reputation, what does that say about the importance of personal image?

That is why now, more than ever before, part of personal leadership is doing what you can to take control of your digital personality and reputation. If you don't at least attempt to take control of it, others will do it for you, and you may not like the result.

Take the 2009 media frenzy that surrounded Tiger Woods, the first billionaire athlete many believed to have the perfect personal image since he turned professional in 1996. That image, crafted through his competitive golf game, the media, rapid online spread, endorsements, and positive word-of-mouth, came crashing down in an instant, and he and his game have never been quite the same since. His image was more than just golf. It was also based heavily on his character, and his behavior away from the game of golf had directly impacted that part of his image (and to what extent over time remains unclear).[4]

Toyota, a company founded in 1950, slowly built its market-leading image in automobile manufacturing based on strong perceptions of quality, safety and excellent design. In the wake of major quality defects that have been linked to a number of fatalities, these perceptions were seriously questioned in 2010 during the largest recall in the history of automobile manufacturing, and the unstable perception of Toyota's finances (once a darling on Wall Street). Combined with production problems created by the 2011 Japanese tsunami and resulting nuclear reactor meltdown in Japan, Toyota still struggles to regain the same image perception it once had.[5,6] According to the J.D. Power & Associates Initial Quality Study, Toyota's brand quality perception dropped from sixth overall (top amongst mass-market producers) to 21st out of 33 brands.[7] The online spread of media stories and discussion boards related to the company's issues has only served to accelerate this change in perception.

Building image and trust is a fragile process done daily, not in a day. Every act, experience, visual and situation, however minor, impacts people's perception of how one's image is defined. Your image lives in the hearts and minds of everyone that comes in contact with you either directly or indirectly. Just as "Elsie" adds value to the Borden image by creating a personal connection with the consumer, the generic brand provides nothing to help create that connection, thereby adding to its long-term "risk" factor. Regardless of the context, people want to be able to comfortably connect with you and trust what you offer.

The longer an image is proactively built, the more likely it will be able to overcome periodic setbacks in perception, which can't be avoided (for example, a perception based on a false statement or accusation made by another). A daily, concerted effort to build an image focused on every detail and personal interaction will help most individuals or organizations overcome these setbacks.

How to Build Your Personal Image.

As you develop and define a sense of who you are and ultimately your personal identity, there are a number of online (and some offline) things that can be done to directly influence others' perception. It's never too late to start (and if you haven't, now would be a good time):

1. Decide how you want people to perceive you, see you, and generally feel about you. What characteristics make you unique? Where do you excel? Whatever you decide, it must be authentic and truly "you," or others will quickly see you as a fraud. I can't think of a person in this world with a better personal image and reputation than my father. One would be hard-pressed to find anyone who would have a negative thing to say about him. This image has been built over the span of his entire life, and he has served as a role model for me for all of mine. However, I am not my father. I can only be me, and any attempt to replicate his image and/or reputation would be seen as something I'm not. That's not to say that he hasn't influenced me because he has, and much of what I am today I owe directly to him. But my personal image has to be mine. It has to represent who I truly am or wish to become, not what I am not or unable to be. Getting there is a process, and everything you do must be part of that.

2. Create an online home (such as a website) that exhibits and provides evidence of your desired image. Remember that the quality of this site directly impacts the quality of your image (something that Starbucks®, Pottery

Barn®, and Apple® realized a long time ago). Provide relevant, value-added information, and most importantly, make sure it's accurate. Factual, grammatical and spelling errors are all killers of a positive personal image. Your online home doesn't have to be business-related. It can be about your interests, hobbies, or activities. It just has to be about you.

3. Create profiles on social media sites (such as Facebook and LinkedIn) that support your desired image. These profiles and the information posted should be both personal and authentic, yet professional as well. Post only information, photos and/or video that support your desired image, versus that which you think are "cool" or "funny" and may actually cause long-term harm to your image. (Think "Rated G," suitable for all audiences.) Also since others can see them, be careful of those you "friend" on these sites. You can become guilty by association by linking yourself to people with poor reputations or undesirable content. There are no prizes for having the most friends. Choose them wisely and regularly monitor their posts in order to be certain that those associated with you online are still supportive of your desired image.

4. Regularly communicate your image on the web through your social networking sites by posting comments to blogs or discussion forums, reviewing books or other relevant media, and asking for feedback, recommendations, testimonials, or comments related to your content (the latter builds credibility, but be careful what you ask for). It's always about quality and not quantity. Don't allow random posts to your sites and only enable comments to specific uploads or posts. Respond to negative comments and initiate a conversation regarding them (keeping the conversation positive and civil).

5. From a professional prospective, create original content that supports your online image through blogging, writing articles, and adding supportive posts to others' work that is in line with your own desired image. Through your life experience you probably know more than you realize. In the offline world, write a book, volunteer your time, lecture or speak to classes and/or people at all levels, and join community-based and professional organizations. It also goes without saying that some "old-school" aspects of image building still apply, such as your style of dress and conduct (personal behavior is still the biggest driver of personal image).

6. Always monitor! Stay on top of your social sites and what your "friends" are doing. What does Google say about you? Check regularly and make sure that what's being presented is accurate and respond to false and negative portrayals in a positive, professional manner. Make sure that the content or sites that you have some control over are near or at the top of a search of your name (utilize one or more of many known search engine optimization techniques available such as the use of "hidden" or invisible keywords throughout your site). Set-up Google Alerts to notify you when your name comes up on the web (over two-thirds of all web searches are conducted through Google).[8] Seek ongoing feedback from those you trust to ensure that what you are communicating is being perceived as intended.

Building an Organizational Image.

From an organizational perspective, the creation of image requires all people, regardless of responsibility, to be properly trained and made aware of how their daily actions ultimately affect perception. They must take control of their personal image as well because markets and consumers today want to know the various "faces" of the organization. Employees at all levels can no longer "hide" behind the company facade, and people expect them to be front and center. The obvious aspects of organizational image building can't be ignored. Product and service quality must be maintained and improved to ensure at least a stable if not growing market share. Physical assets, buildings and grounds must be kept immaculate. And basically, the entire customer experience must be regularly evaluated and updated to reflect changes in customer needs and wants.

People often ask me how to create and maintain a competitive advantage through organizational image today in an environment marked by rapid changes in technology, fluid delivery systems, global competition, real-time communication through the Internet, and instant (and often brutal) customer "experience" reports through social media sites. Although I do think it's becoming ever more difficult to maintain an advantage, I have a solution.

The Golden Answer.

A day doesn't go by that I don't hear about someone bemoaning a poor customer service experience. In fact, I believe customer service has gotten so bad that some people seem to just expect it. We, as customers, have collectively lowered our bar so much that we have become ever more tolerant of being treated poorly. So here's my "golden" competitive advantage answer for building your organizational (or personal) image: Regardless of rapidly changing market conditions, advances in technology, or whatever else people struggle with to stay current, you don't need to create or invent the next greatest thing to stay ahead of the competition. Simply build a total culture of above-and-beyond service, and this will immediately place you ahead of most, if not all, of the competition.

It begins with personal leadership. You become successful by helping others get what they want. Your attitude matters most when dealing with people. Your attitude sells. Go beyond the Golden Rule. In other words, treat people BETTER than you would want to be treated. As a kid, my father regularly told me that if you borrow something from someone, always return it in better condition than when you initially received it. Then others will always be willing to help you again if you need it. When people come to you for what you provide, they are investing their time (and possibly some of their money). Give them back something of greater value. If people believe you truly care and are all about taking care of them first and foremost, they will give you their business, even if your products and services don't have all of the latest bells and whistles.

Bottom line: Regardless of anything else, people's perception of an experience still comes down to how they feel.

I have developed something of an obsession with Mont Blanc® pens and products. Although there are many other excellent pens and leather products out there (even some with better features), I had become loyal not only to Mont Blanc, but also to one particular boutique. I've purchased merchandise at a number of different Mont Blanc boutiques across the country, but only the store in Oak Brook, Illinois truly stands out (this store has since been consolidated into the downtown Chicago store). When I visited this particular store, not only did my service representative there take care of my wants (this really doesn't classify as a needs purchase), she went way above and beyond EVERY time. Each time I made a purchase, she would send me a very nice, handwritten note in beautiful calligraphy thanking me for my purchase. She sent me cards on special days like birthdays and Christmas and often for no particular reason but just to say that she hoped all was going well, all in the same striking penmanship. She quickly resolved any purchase issues and often tossed in free "extras," such as pen and pad refills. She took the time to make me feel special and show that my commitment of money was worth it. No other person at any other store (Mont Blanc or otherwise) had invested this much time into my personal satisfaction. As a result, she had my permanent loyalty. She obviously cared about her personal image, and after receiving the news that she was going to be "downsized," she even took the time to inform me of the closing and personally connected me with my new Chicago-based representative. Now that is service and personal leadership. Given the chance, she is the kind of person I would hire in an instant.

People value most how you make them feel. They will ultimately act based on those feelings. So give them something worth their investment of time and money. If you make them feel special, they will reward you with their long-term loyalty. By proactively building a personal image of service to others, you will create a sustainable competitive advantage in image, despite whatever other label you may have been given.

So I guess the delivery driver was wrong. What's on the outside needs to match what's on the inside. Cows aren't always cows after all.

Fighting Off the Purple People Eaters

- ☐ Ask your "sounding board" for an honest assessment of how others perceive you. Is their feedback in line with how you want to be viewed? If not, perhaps it's time for a change, one way or another.

- ☐ People naturally deviate towards that which is reliable. Be reliable.

- ☐ List five people that you believe have "great lives." Why do you think so? What do they have in common? How are they different?

CHAPTER 9

The Good, the Bad, and the Beauty of It.

The principles you live by create the world you live in; if you change the principles you live by, you will change your world.

– Blaine Lee

Good Versus Bad.

As a kid, I used to love reading *Mad Magazine*, especially the "Spy vs. Spy" comic, where one spy was always trying to outdo the other. The characters were identical in appearance, other than one was all white in color while the other was all black. Perhaps an insinuation of good versus evil? Not sure. But this concept sort of reflects how I view technology today—two sides of the same thing, nearly always in competition with each other.

Technology has transformed our lives, often in positive (and previously unimagined) ways. It has the power to enhance business activity, facilitate financial transactions, expedite communication, provide exceptionally realistic visuals (while it entertains), and transport us to distant worlds. However, if left unchecked, technology also possesses the potential to negatively affect how we live and interact as human beings. Unfortunately, this "bad side" already seems to have engulfed younger generations and is rapidly spreading into older ones (including my own). We are now witnessing the impact on a variety of social norms and customs. Behaviors that were once considered unacceptable now seem to be fairly common.

For example, consider the following:

- **Too much public disclosure.** Regardless of its direct impact on one's personal identity, the Internet has opened the door to decreased privacy. For instance, most of us have likely witnessed people who seem to have no problem carrying on very personal conversations through texting, email, tweeting and social media. It's easy to judge others and assume "I would never do that," but have you ever sent a personal email, picture, cartoon or joke to someone that, if it appeared with your name on the front page of the newspaper, would mortify you? Also, with ever-improving cameras on smartphones, your actions are always under scrutiny (thank you, Moore's Law). During a recent trip to Las Vegas, I saw a t-shirt with the saying, "What happens in Vegas, stays on YouTube." Like it or not, what you once believed to be private is now probably sitting on a server somewhere. Once something enters the Internet, it tends to stay there, and we may have little choice regarding who views it.

• **Changing "rules" for social manners.** Situations once deemed quiet, such as face-to-face conversations, meetings, interviews, classes, weddings, funerals and a variety of other instances, are now routinely interrupted by the indiscriminate usage of cell phones. And a growing number of people now seem more accepting of the practice. What's worse: when people *answer* their phones regardless of circumstance. Nearly constant emailing and texting to others during actual face-to-face interactions has also become much more common.

• **Reduced face-to-face interaction.** The ease with which technology allows us to communicate can also create a splurge of texts and email. Sometimes the message itself gets lost in a sea of messages; the back-and-forth of an email or text thread can actually waste more time than just making a simple phone call. This practice opens the door to confusion and misunderstanding due to the lack of proper context and verbal/non-verbal cues, provides a tempting platform for people to say nearly anything without having to actually face the recipient (thus hiding behind their words), and as a lawyer once told me, creates "evidence." I once spent ten minutes watching my teenage daughter and four of her friends sitting in my living room texting and not saying a single word to each other. Texting is easy and immediate, but like with most things, there's a price for the convenience.

• **An inability to disconnect.** We love our smartphones and Bluetooth® devices. But when do they become extra appendages we can't seem to live without? They have certainly changed the workplace, often in positive ways. But at what point do they blur the lines between work and personal life?

• **A condensed life.** Through text messaging, Twitter, and Facebook posts, people have become accustomed to communicating in short, abbreviated statements, which leads to the sharing of immediate, random thoughts (i.e., "theater popcorn—yum!") and "checking-in" when they visit places (thus making everyone in their respective network aware of their current location). When daily life is condensed into short bursts of text and tiny amounts of time, the result can be decreased attention spans. Research has shown that young, developing brains can become more habituated than adult brains to constantly switching tasks and less able to sustain attention. According to Michael Rich, an associate professor at Harvard Medical School and executive director of the Center on Media and Child Health in Boston, "Their brains are rewarded, not for staying on task, but for jumping to the next thing."[1] Patricia Greenfield, a professor at UCLA, looked at more than 50 studies of technology's effects on children and found that technology appears to be damaging critical reasoning and reducing attention span, thus leaving children less skilled at concentrating on a particular point for very long.[2]

• **Poor writing skills.** The new form of abbreviated, acronym-laden writing has directly affected individual writing skills. We've all heard people in business, education, or the media—maybe we've said it ourselves—bemoan the lack of writing skills in people today, and ample evidence can be seen all around us. This lack of skills isn't just reflected in email or other forms of online communication. Like many professors, I've received numerous term papers riddled with texting acronyms instead of complete thoughts. Needless to say, these types of oversights negatively impact student grades.

- **The costs of immediate (24/7) feedback.** The results of many decisions can take time to play out, and sometimes a "mental processing" or "cooling off" period is the best thing for solving a conflict. But with continuous updates, daily opinion polls, unlimited information on the fly, and constant connection, patience doesn't seem to be the virtue it once was. This new form of technological immediacy can lead to the rapid spread of "bad" information, reviews, and growing discontent. It's tough enough to do the hard things and make difficult decisions that require time in order to achieve desired outcomes—and even tougher when people expect "instant."

- **Difficulty differentiating "real" versus "unreal."** Most of us have probably caught ourselves being intrigued by the lifelike qualities and stupendous special effects of video games, even if we don't play ourselves and are simply wandering through Target®. Yet is it no wonder that many are increasingly concerned—with good reason—about the apparent decrease in the imagination and creativity of children? Video game sales now surpass those of box office franchises such as *Star Wars* and *Harry Potter*.[3] The biggest difference, however, may be the shift in how we spend our time. An occasional two-hour movie seems like a small chunk of time versus the hours, maybe even days at a time, that some of our kids spend gaming.

• **Identity Theft.** These are two words that were never heard together in normal conversation until the advent of the personal computer. Enough said.

I could go on, but I'm sure you get the point. With the huge amount of positives that come with technology, there are an equal amount of negatives. We need to be proactively *aware* of these negatives and how they may ultimately affect our lives, our desired outcomes, and others around us. More computing power exists today in a simple musical birthday card than in the entire world 60 years ago. If Moore's Law continues to hold true, and computing power/capacity continues to double every 24 months (or less), one can only imagine what wonders or possible problems might be in store for us.

I've had to learn through personal experience (again, often by making mistakes) what works for me in terms of using technology and what doesn't. Life is complicated enough, and it's not smart or safe to assume technology will always make it easier. I've learned to not just automatically accept all new technologies that come along and to proactively assess whether they will serve to help me become more productive and effective. We learn by trying, but effective personal leadership dictates that you must be willing to evaluate something on your own and not allow yourself to be drawn into it just because everyone is doing or using it. In his book, *I'm Working On That*, William Shatner writes:

> *And that's kind of the way it happens with technology, isn't it? It's seductive and embraces us until we get used to it and can't do without it... At first it's a luxury, the domain of early adopters, and then after a while we need this stuff. In fact the reason we get so upset when computers don't work is because we've become so reliant on them. If we weren't reliant, we wouldn't give a damn. We wouldn't even know they were broken.*[4]

Time to Shift Gears.

Most parents can probably relate to this scenario (teens too): The parent tries to share with the teen something of value that's been learned through years of personal experience (let's call it wisdom). The teen responds with an eye roll of disregard, some kind of utterance like "whatever," or simply just ignores the parent. The parent becomes a little frustrated and presses harder. The teen presses back. Some kind of "discussion" ensues that escalates into something else. The word "disrespect" is either thought or spoken. Sharing time is over (although it may have never really started).

Most parents I know would love to be able to pass on all their collective wisdom to children who would not only listen, but also take this wisdom to heart and not repeat the same mistakes. I wasn't one of those of kids (and I may have even made life a little more difficult for my parents than most), but I am now one of those parents, who, ironically, wants people to listen. Although some of what I have written has a parental overtone (from the experience of many personal failures combined with the insights learned from those much wiser), if there is one lesson that I wish people would take to heart, including my own children, it would be one related to the use of money.

Money 101.

What discussion on personal leadership would be complete without at least some focus on personal financial management? A quick perusal of the shelves at any bookstore or an online search will yield millions of books on the topic (perhaps a slight exaggeration, but you get my point). Whether it's a snowball strategy to eliminate existing debt, an investment scheme to maximize returns, or a method to enhance income by selling off extra stuff on eBay®, there are endless ideas put forth by a great many people.

My insight into the area of personal finance comes directly as a result of personal experience. In fact, I've come to believe I now hold the ultimate secret to financial prosperity—a philosophy that required a large number of financial missteps and most of my life to finally figure out. Before I share this little gem of insight, I must confess that as a marketing-minded individual, this insight tends to run contrary to the very nature of my efforts to position and promote products to the masses. It also runs contrary to what has become considered "normal" behavior by a majority of people, companies, and our government. It's a lesson that I had to learn both through personal experience and the experiences of those close to me. It came to me one day as a life-changing epiphany—a realization that my current financial choices were unsustainable and something had to change. I believe personal financial success can be summed up in this one, simple pearl of wisdom:

Spend less than you make.

Yes, we've heard this phrase before. But how many of us actually put it into practice? I'm convinced that for most of us (as individuals and as corporate and government entities), sustainable long-term financial success rests with this basic principle. I also know this practice may be a lot easier to *say* than to actually *do*. For many, this philosophy requires a total life paradigm shift—one that includes a commitment to changing bad spending habits and making better long- and short-term decisions related to the use of limited resources. Many of the ideas suggested by others will help with this process, but none will ultimately be successful until you start spending less than you make. I suppose an alternative strategy would be to raise your income to a level greater than your spending, but for most of us, reducing the amount we spend is probably easier, especially given today's economic reality.

Everyone I know who has changed spending behavior in this way has, **over time**, enjoyed reduced debt, greater flexibility in decision-making, a growth in savings, and (especially) less stress. Changing your daily, incremental spending behaviors with the intent of spending less will, **over time**, help you become more self-sufficient and free to do the things you "want" versus what you "have to."

In his book, *You Don't Know Me from Adam*, Adam Carroll (also author of *Winning the Money Game*) shares what he calls the Four Legacies we must leave future generations.

His philosophy begins with creating Financial Freedom, which leads to Time Freedom, because people with money generally have more time. Time Freedom leads to Relationship Freedom, or the ability to spend quality time with those you wish. Finally, Relationship Freedom leads to Service Freedom, or the ability to be of service to others in a way that gives you purpose.[5]

Notice that this entire process begins with creating Financial Freedom. The freedom created by having control of your daily financial choices must start with making the decision to spend less than you make. Many people do not have financial freedom (and thus struggle with realizing the other levels of freedom). Instead they have developed just the opposite—financial stress. Money is a leading, growing source of stress for Americans. More than three out of every four American families are now in debt today, according to the Federal Reserve's Survey of Consumer Finances.[6] According to a study by the American Psychological Association, three-fourths of the respondents cited money as a significant source of stress in their lives. The *Stress in America* survey also points to a looming national health crisis caused by the stress created as a result of money-related (76 percent) and work-related (70 percent) issues.[7]

Debt creates financial bondage which in turn creates stress. The only real way to reduce debt and the stress which results from it is to make the decision to regularly spend less than you make. Remember, most goals are achieved daily, not in a single day. Your debt, like nearly everything else in your life, was more than likely accumulated over time, so this philosophy requires a permanent change in daily spending behavior.

80 Percent Action.

I'm a strong believer that effective organizational leadership begins with effective personal leadership. The choices, decisions and consequences in each context are not mutually exclusive, but mutually connected. Leadership occurs when the behavior of someone is influenced with the intent of achieving something else in an ethical way. The first "someone" in the sequence must be you. We must be able to make creative decisions and visualize the path towards success, remain focused and allow the necessary time for decisions to play out, possess the work ethic, motivation and discipline to do what it takes, and assume responsibility for both our physical and digital selves in order to successfully lead others (as well as establish the credibility necessary to gain their confidence).

Most of what I've written is focused almost exclusively on process and personal behavior. I believe that true leadership is based on 20 percent knowledge and 80 percent action. In other words, successful leadership is far less about what you know and far more about what you do (or sometimes don't do). Since the amount of information today is increasing at an exponential rate, strong leaders must know how to locate required information when needed, how to evaluate the credibility of such information, and how to effectively apply it when making decisions.

In the spirit of one of my favorite books, John Maxwell's *21 Irrefutable Laws of Leadership*, I have developed my own laws over the years that have worked well for me. Many of these ideas began as personal leadership laws that have since carried over to my other organizational roles:

- **Always think "Big Picture."** I will develop genuine holistic problem-solving skills, think creatively, and visualize all aspects of solutions before implemented.

- **Be passionate about what I am going to do, and then do it.** To build trust in others (which is ultimately necessary to accomplish anything), I will always exhibit a high degree of passion, energy, honesty, integrity, and follow-through.

- **Never expect more than I am willing to do myself.** I cannot expect people to go the extra mile, put in overtime, or do whatever it takes to be successful if I am not willing to do the same on a regular, consistent basis.

- **Always be fair and balanced.** I will strive to never show favoritism and always treat others equally regardless of status or position. Being fair and equal to everyone builds trust and loyalty and creates a sense of value.

- **Be approachable at all times.** People must feel like they can come to me when they need or want to do so. I will not set up any form of "gatekeeper" to control access to me, which would thus impede communication.

- **Manage through interaction.** I will make an effort to walk around and interact with others on a regular basis to help keep me connected to the environment I am leading. I want others to see me as approachable and accessible.

- **Be consistent.** I will remain committed to staying even-tempered and displaying stability, thus modeling and promoting consistency in the decision-making process. People will always know what to expect, which will serve to minimize anxiety.

- **Surround myself with great people.** I will surround myself with and help to develop others who possess and exhibit strengths greater than myself. A good leader acknowledges weaknesses and offsets them by partnering with others who are strong in those areas.

- **Share responsibility.** I will truly delegate responsibility, which serves to build value within people. I will not micro-manage, yet I will continue to provide support when needed.

- **Give lots of credit—take very little.** As a leader, I am the ship's navigator, not its engine. I will never put myself in a position to take something of value from the people I am leading which would only serve to devalue their efforts and kill their motivation.

What Will Be in Your Dash?

A tombstone (a monument to one's life) usually contains the name and "life years" of someone no longer living. Although the inscription typically focuses on the years when a person was born and subsequently passed away, a person's life is actually represented by the "dash" in between (i.e., 1964 – 2042). This dash represents the bulk of our lives—the succession of joys, sorrows, successes, failures, and other experiences. Although tombstones don't tell the full story, the "dash" is where life actually happens. If you could write the story of your dash, how would it read? Would it be full of regrets for all of the things that you did or didn't do? Or would it be a tribute to all that you attempted to do, be and accomplish while you were alive?

The choice is yours. Whether or not you are living your desired dash or just dashing your way through life comes down to personal leadership. Life is framed by a start and finish. The story of your dash will come down to the choices made within your limited time.

Kris Allen, winner of the eighth season of *American Idol*, sang these words in his first released single:

> *Yeah, we gotta start lookin' at the hands*
> *of the time we've been given*
> *If this is all we got, then we gotta start thinkin'*
> *If every second counts on a clock that's tickin'*
> *gotta live like we're dying*
> *We only got 86 400 seconds in a day to*
> *turn it all around or to throw it all away..."*[8]

Many people have good intentions but aren't as good with actions. They often act as if they have all the time in the world left to get things done. But what if you knew exactly when your time was up? Would you live life any differently? Would you make different choices? The decision to take control and be a proactive personal leader is ultimately yours. So make it. The rest of your life begins today.

- ☐ Ask: "What do I really want? When I reach the end of my life, will I be glad that I got it or did it?"

- ☐ In what situations do you feel uptight, anxious, stressed, or maybe even sick to your stomach? Avoid these situations when possible or remove the context that causes them.

- ☐ Learn from adversity. It affects us all, and we must deal with it on our own, like the newly-hatched chick which must break out of the egg on its own or die. But something positive can be gleaned from each and every situation if you look for it.

NOTES

Forethought

1. Heath, C. and Heath D. (2008). *Made to Stick.* New York, NY: Random House, Inc.

Chapter 1

1. Zagursky, E. (2010, July 14). *Professor Discusses America's Creativity Crisis in Newsweek.* Retrieved November 18, 2010, from the College of William & Mary website: http://www.wm.edu/news/stories/2010/professor-discusses-americas-creativity-crisis-in-newsweek-123.php
2. Bronson, P. (2010, July 10). *The Creativity Crisis.* Retrieved November 18, 2010, from the Newsweek website: http://www.newsweek.com/2010/07/10/the-creativity-crisis.print.html
3. (2010, May 18). *IBM 2010 Global CEO Study: Creativity Selected as Most Crucial Factor for Future Success.* Retrieved November 18, 2010, from the IBM website: http://www-03.ibm.com/press/us/en/pressrelease/31670.wss
4. *Statistics on Patents.* Retrieved January 21, 2011, from the World Intellectual Property Organization website: http://www.wipo.int/ipstats/en/statistics/patents
5. Barboza, D. (2010, October 6). *China Poised to Lead World in Patent Filings.* Retrieved February 4, 2011, from the *New York Times* website: http://economix.blogs.nytimes.com/2010/10/06/china-poised-to-lead-world-in-patent-filings
6. Fox, J., & Fox, R. (2006). *Exploring the Nature of Creativity.* Dubuque, IA: Kendall Hunt Publishing Company.
7. Paustian, A. (1997). *Imagine! Enhancing Your Critical Thinking and Problem-Solving Skills.* Upper Saddle River, NJ: Prentice Hall.

8. *Francium.* Retrieved January 25, 2011, from the Elementymology & Elements Multidict website: http://elements.vanderkrogt.net/element.php?sym=fr

9. Bellis, M. *The History of Commercial Deodorants.* Retrieved January 28, 2011, from the About.Com Inventors website: http://inventors.about.com/od/dstartinventions/a/deodorants.htm

10. (2004, September 20) *Fred Smith on the Birth of FedEx.* Retrieved January 21, 2011, from the Bloomberg *Businessweek* website: http://www.businessweek.com/magazine/content/04_38/b3900032_mz072.htm

11. (1996). *Thomas Edison Quotes.* Retrieved February 6, 2011, from the Thomas Edison.com website: http://www.thomasedison.com/quotes.html

12. (2007, December 26). *Invention of the Telephone Switch.* Retrieved January 29, 2011, from the Strowger website: http://www.strowger.com/about-us/strowger-invention-of-telephone-switch.html

13. *John Dunlop.* Retrieved January 29, 2011, from the Great Idea Finder website: http://www.ideafinder.com/history/inventors/dunlop.htm

14. Suddath, C. (2009, June 23). *A Brief History of Kodachrome.* Retrieved January 29, 2011, from the *Time Magazine* website: http://www.time.com/time/arts/article/0,8599,1906503,00.html

15. *Female Inventors–Hedy Lamarr.* Retrieved January 29, 2011, from the Inventors website: http://www.inventions.org/culture/female/lamarr.html

16. *Edison's Miracle of Light.* Retrieved January 29, 2011, from the Public Broadcasting Service (PBS) website: http://www.pbs.org/wgbh/amex/edison/filmmore/description.html

17. *The Apollo Program.* Retrieved May 15, 2010, from the National Aeronautics and Space Administration (NASA) website: http://history.nasa.gov/apollo.html

18. *The Quartz Watch.* Retrieved February 6, 2011, from the Smithsonian website: http://invention.smithsonian.org/centerpieces/quartz/inventors/index.html

19. Tang, K. (2010, September 28). *Flat Panel TV History.* Retrieved February 6, 2011, from the eHow website: http://www.ehow.com/facts_7250075_flat-panel-tv-history.html

20. *World's Fair History.* Retrieved January 27, 2011, from the EXPO Museum website: http://www.expomuseum.com

Chapter 2

1. Whitfield, S.E. & Roddenberry G. (1968). *The Making of Star Trek.* New York, NY: Ballantine Books.

2. *List of Star Trek Races.* Retrieved October 14, 2011, from Wikipedia, the Free Encyclopedia website: http://en.wikipedia.org/wiki/List_of_Star_Trek_races

3. Paustian, T., Personal Communication, October 9, 2011.

4. *Box Office History for Star Trek Movies.* Retrieved October 13, 2011, from the Numbers website: http://www.the-numbers.com/movies/series/StarTrek.php

5. *Motion Pictures By Independent Filmakers.* Retrieved October 13, 2011, from the American United Entertainment website: http://www.americanunitedent.com/ifi.htm

6. *The Blair Witch Project (1999) Trivia.* Retrieved October 13, 2011, from the Internet Movie Database (IMDB) website: http://www.imdb.com/title/tt0185937/trivia

7. *In Saturn's Shadow.* Retrieved October 17, 2011, from the NASA Jet Propulsion Laboratory website: http://photojournal.jpl.nasa.gov/catalog/PIA08329

8. *Inventors of the Modern Computer.* Retrieved October 18, 2011, from the About.com Inventors website: http://inventors.about.com/library/weekly/aa121598.htm

9. Salter, C. (2009, June). *Through the Fire.* Fast Company, 60.

10. Jones, D. *"Punched Cards."* Retrieved October 2, 2011, from the University of Iowa website: http://www.divms.uiowa.edu/~jones/cards/history.html

11. Moore, G.E. (1965, April 19). *Cramming More Components onto Integrated Circuits.* Retrieved October 18, 2011, from the Intel website: ftp://download.intel.com/museum/Moores_Law/Articles-Press_Releases/Gordon_Moore_1965_Article.pdf

12. Fries, A. (2010, January 19). *The Dynamic Duo: Imagination + Knowledge.* Retrieved September 29, 2011, from the Psychology Today website: http://www.psychologytoday.com/blog/the-power-daydreaming/201001/the-dynamic-duo-imagination-knowledge

13. Handel, A. (Producer), & Jones, J. (Director). (2005). *How William Shatner Changed the World.* [Film]. United States: Allumination Filmworks.

Chapter 3

1. Heath, C. and Heath D. (2008). *Made to Stick.* New York, NY: Random House, Inc.

Chapter 4

1. Marantz, Steve (2002). *History of the World Series – 1997.* Retrieved February 16, 2010, from *Sporting News* website: http://www.sportingnews.com/archives/worldseries/1997.html

Chapter 5

1. *The American Heritage Dictionary of the English Language,* 4th Edition. (2010). Boston, MA: Houghton Mifflin Harcourt Publishing Company.

2. Maxwell, J. (1998). *The 21 Irrefutable Laws of Leadership.* Nashville, TN: Thomas Nelson Publishers.

3. *Gazette Classics: Kurt Warner File* (Select Articles from Gazette Text Archives, 1998-2008). Retrieved November 4, 2010, from the WordPress website: http://lookinginatiowa.wordpress.com/gazette-classics-kurt-warner-file

4. Belle, A. *Kurt Warner: Biography, Facts, and Stats.* Retrieved November 4, 2010, from the FreeResource website: http://www.thefreeresource.com/kurt-warner-biography-facts-and-stats

5. Warner, K. & Silver, M. (2000). *All Things Possible.* New York, NY: HarperCollins Publishers.

6. *James Dyson.* Retrieved November 5, 2010, from the Great Idea Finder website: http://www.ideafinder.com/history/inventors/dyson.htm

7. *Chester F. Carlson.* Retrieved November 5, 2010, from the Great Idea Finder website: http://www.ideafinder.com/history/inventors/carlson.htm

8. *Seussville: Dr. Seuss's Biography.* Retrieved November 5, 2010, from the Seussville website: http://www.seussville.com/#/author

9. Carlin, G. (1997). *Brain Droppings.* New York, NY: Hyperion.

Chapter 6

1. Organ, D., Podsakoff, P. & MacKenzie, S. (2006). *Organizational Citizenship Behavior.* Thousand Oaks, CA: Sage Publications, Inc.

2. Carroll, A. (2012). *You Don't Know Me from Adam.* Des Moines, IA: Four Legacies Publishing.

3. Zabloski, J. (1996). *The 25 Most Common Problems in Business (and How Jesus Solved Them).* Nashville, TN: Broadman & Holman Publishers.

4. *Babe Ruth.* Retrieved December 3, 2010, from the Baseball-Reference website: http://www.baseball-reference.com/players/r/ruthba01.shtml

5. Rosner, B. (2005, February 25). *Working Wounded: Getting Pink Slipped.* Retrieved December 3, 2010, from the ABC News website: http://abcnews.go.com/Business/Working Wounded/story?id=547848

6. Beals, G. (1999). *The Biography of Thomas Edison.* Retrieved December 3, 2010, from the Thomas Edison website: http://www.thomasedison.com/biography.html

7. *Michael Jordan Quotes.* Retrieved December 3, 2010, from the Brainy Quote website: http://www.brainyquote.com/quotes/quotes/m/michaeljor127660.html

8. *Lee Iacocca.* Retrieved December 3, 2010, from the Encyclopedia of World Biography website: http://www.notable biographies.com/Ho-Jo/Iacocca-Lee.html

9. Ziskin, L. (Producer), Williams, B. (Producer), & Oz, F. (Director). (1991). *What About Bob?* [Motion Picture]. United States: Touchstone Pictures.

10. *Holy Bible, New Century Version.* (2003). Nashville, TN: Thomas Nelson, Inc.

Chapter 7

1. *The Apollo Program.* Retrieved May 15, 2010, from the National Aeronautics and Space Administration (NASA) website: http://history.nasa.gov/apollo.html

2. Haake, A. (2009, July). Time Machine – March 1962. *Popular Mechanics,* 21.

3. *The Alamo - History.* Retrieved May 18, 2010, from the Official Alamo website: http://www.thealamo.org/history.html

4. Gruver, E. (1997). The Lombardi Sweep. *The Coffin Corner*, Vol. 19, No. 5. http://www.profootballresearchers.org/Coffin_Corner/19-05-712.pdf

Chapter 8

1. *The Devil Wears Prada.* Retrieved August 3, 2011, from the IMDb (Internet Movie Database) website: http://www.imdb.com/title/tt0458352/quotes

2. Zickuhr, K. (2010, December 16). *Generations Online in 2010.* Retrieved July 25, 2011, from the Pew Internet Research website: http://pewinternet.org/Reports/2010/Generations-2010/Overview.aspx

3. Protess, B., Rusli, E., & Craig, S. (2011, March 31). *Buffet's Handling of Deputy Baffles Some Experts.* Retrieved June 21, 2011, from the *New York Times* website: http://dealbook.nytimes.com/2011/03/31/buffetts-handling-of-deputy-baffles-some-experts/?partner=rss&emc=rss

4. Bissinger, B. (2010, February). *Tiger in the Rough.* Retrieved July 27, 2011, from the *Vanity Fair* website: http://www.vanityfair.com/culture/features/2010/02/tiger-woods-201002?printable=true

5. (2010, February 24). *Toyota's Humbling Fall.* Retrieved July 27, 2011, from the CBS News website: http://www.cbsnews.com/stories/2010/02/24/eveningnews/main6240051.shtml

6. (2010). *Toyota's Fall is Speeding Out of Control.* Retrieved July 27, 2011, from the *Motor Trend* website: http://www.printfriendly.com/print/v2?url=http%3A%2F%2Fblogs.motortrend.com%2Ftoyotas-fall-is-speeding-out-of-control-2592.html

7. Jensen, C. (2010, June 18). Toyota's Image Falls in J.D. Power Survey, *New York Times,* sec. B, 5.

8. (2011, July 13). *comScore Releases June 2011 U.S. U.S. Search Engine Rankings.* Retrieved July 27, 2011, from the PR Newswire website: http://www.prnewswire.com/news-releases/comscore-releases-june-2011-us-search-engine-rankings-125513223.html

Chapter 9

1. Richtel, M. (2010, November 21). *Growing Up Digital, Wired for Distraction.* Retrieved November 26, 2011, from the *New York Times* website: http://www.nytimes.com/2010/11/21/technology/21brain.html?pagewanted=all

2. Lister, J. (2009, January 30). *Technology Has Mixed Effects on Child Development, Research Suggests.* Retrieved November 26, 2011, from the Info Packets website: http://www.infoPackets.com/news/technology/it/2009/20090130_technology_has_mixed_effects_on_child_development_research_suggests.htm

3. Snider, M. (2011, November 18). 'Call of Duty' sells $775M in 5 days, rivals movie giants. *USA Today,* 1A.

4. Shatner, W. & Walter, C. (2004). *I'm Working on That.* New York, NY: Pocket Books, Inc.

5. Carroll, A. (2012). *You Don't Know Me from Adam.* Des Moines, IA: Four Legacies Publishing.

6. Soong, J. (2010). *The Debt-Stress Connection.* Retrieved November 26, 2011, from the Web MD website: http://www.webmd.com/balance/features/the-debt-stress-connection

7. Hickey, J. (2010, November 10). *Stress Over Money, Work, Economy Top the List for Americans.* Retrieved November 26, 2011, from the ABC News website: http://www.abcnews.go.com/Business/American-psychological-association-2010-stress-america-survey/story?id=12108276#.TtG9fmBR6CY

8. *Live Like We're Dying* lyrics. Retrieved December 7, 2011, from the MetroLyrics website: http://www.metrolyrics.com/live-like-were-dying-lyrics-kris-allen.html

Additional resources from Anthony Paustian may be found on his website at:

www.adpaustian.com